Mindfulness Training

Ensure a Deep Sleep With Guided Meditation and Self Heal Your Mind and Calm Your Body

(An Easy Guide to Quickly Relieve Stress and Feel Present in Everyday Situations)

Keith Smith

Published by Rob Miles

© **Keith Smith**

All Rights Reserved

Mindfulness Training: Ensure a Deep Sleep With Guided Meditation and Self Heal Your Mind and Calm Your Body (An Easy Guide to Quickly Relieve Stress and Feel Present in Everyday Situations)

ISBN 978-1-989990-97-1

All rights reserved. No part of this guide may be reproduced in any form without permission in writing from the publisher except in the case of brief quotations embodied in critical articles or reviews.

Legal & Disclaimer

The information contained in this book is not designed to replace or take the place of any form of medicine or professional medical advice. The information in this book has been provided for educational and entertainment purposes only.

The information contained in this book has been compiled from sources deemed reliable, and it is accurate to the best of the Author's knowledge; however, the Author cannot guarantee its accuracy and validity and cannot be held liable for any errors or omissions. Changes are periodically made to this book. You must consult your doctor or get professional medical advice before using any of the suggested remedies, techniques, or information in this book.

Upon using the information contained in this book, you agree to hold harmless the Author from and against any damages, costs, and expenses, including any legal fees potentially resulting from the application of any of the information provided by this guide. This disclaimer applies to any damages or injury caused by the use and application, whether directly or indirectly, of any advice or information presented, whether for breach of contract, tort, negligence, personal injury, criminal intent, or under any other cause of action.

You agree to accept all risks of using the information presented inside this book. You need to consult a professional medical practitioner in order to ensure you are both able and healthy enough to participate in this program.

Table of Contents

INTRODUCTION 1

CHAPTER 1: MINDFULNESS 101 3

CHAPTER 2: THE SCIENCE BEHIND MINDFULNESS MEDITATION 21

CHAPTER 3: UNDERSTANDING MINDFULNESS 34

CHAPTER 4: MINDFULNESS MEDITATION 41

CHAPTER 5: PREPARATION: SETTING AND BODY MECHANICS 50

CHAPTER 6: MEDITATIONS 57

CHAPTER 7: MINDFULNESS IN EVERYDAY LIFE 69

CHAPTER 8: CONCEPT OF MINDFULNESS 74

CHAPTER 9: WHY PRACTICE MINDFULNESS? 85

CHAPTER 10: MINDFULNESS TECHNIQUE #1: THE CAMERA 95

CHAPTER 11: UNDERSTANDING MINDFULNESS 101

CHAPTER 12: BODY SCAN MEDITATION 112

CHAPTER 13: MEDITATION PRINCIPLES 124

CHAPTER 14: STRESS AND FLOW STATE 136

CHAPTER 15: PRACTICING GUIDED MINDFULNESS MEDITATION WITH AUDIO VISUAL STIMULATION. 152

CHAPTER 16: BODY AND MIND AS ONE 160

- CHAPTER 17: BENEFITS OF MINDFULNESS 163
- CHAPTER 18: BEING MINDFUL OF THOUGHTS 167
- CHAPTER 19: PRACTICING YOUR METACOGNITIVE SKILLS 170
- CHAPTER 20: FIVE PRECEPTS 174
- CHAPTER 21: REACHING WEIGHT LOSS GOALS 181
- CHAPTER 22: HOW MEDITATION CAN CHANGE YOUR LIFE 187
- CONCLUSION 200

Introduction

Stress is everywhere these days. The non-stop work culture we seem to have built for ourselves has led us to adopting stress as a necessity and as a point of pride. All of our business role models, from Elon Musk to Jeff Bezos, talk about how work is the most important thing and that stress is just something that comes with the territory.

Well, they're not entirely wrong. If you're working to build something in your life, you will encounter stress. However, to think that it has to belong in your life and that it is necessary to get things done is unvarnished nonsense. The truth is that stress is pretty much one of the worst things you can subject yourself to.

Some level of stress is necessary in order to get things done. For example, if you're preparing for an interview or a test of some kind, you need a little fear and stress to push you to prepare for it and do well on it. This kind of stress gives you a little boost and ensures you dot every i and cross every t.

The problem starts occurring when it crosses this line and begins to affect you physically and eventually mentally. Your mind and body are connected to one another and anything that debilitates one is sure to affect the other equally. Constant exposure to high levels of stress ruins your quality of life and eventually manifests as physical disease as well.

Chapter 1: Mindfulness 101

Mindfulness practice is getting more and more popular nowadays, especially in the field of psychology. More and more mental health professionals recommend the daily practice of mindfulness to their patients. However, mindfulness is not a new concept. In fact, it has been around for 2,500 years.

Mindfulness is the core element Buddhist practices such as Vipassana, anapanasati, and sattipatthana. Dr. Jon Kabat-Zinn popularized it in the West when he developed the MBSR or Mindfulness-based Stress Reduction technique. This technique is now widely used by medical professionals, hospitals, medical centers, and health maintenance organizations. Kabat-Zinn learned the mindfulness technique from Zen masters like Seung Sahn and Thich Nhat Hanh.

What is mindfulness, really? Well, mindfulness is the gentle effort to be incessantly present with experience. Mindfulness is paying attention with purpose. It is a state of open and active attention to the present moment. When you are being mindful, you observe your actions, feelings, and thoughts from a distance without judgment.

The regular practice of meditation has a number of scientifically backed benefits, including:

Mindfulness lowers stress.

Research shows that mindfulness can reduce stress substantially. It helps control the production of stress hormones called cortisol.

It helps you know yourself more.

Mindfulness meditation helps you get to know yourself more. It helps you objectively analyze yourself and it helps you get to know your feelings more.

It improves your cognitive function.

Studies show that practicing mindfulness meditation on a regular basis helps improve your cognitive function. A research shows that college students who practiced mindfulness scored better in the GRE than those who did not.

A study conducted in 2010 also shows that mindfulness help improves the memory. This study shows the military officers who practiced mindfulness have better memory than those who didn't.

A study conducted at the University of California – Los Angeles shows that people who practice mindfulness meditation for more than a year has bigger amounts of gyrification, or the folds in the brain's cortex. These extra folds help practitioners process information faster than regular folks. These extra folds also improve your decision-making skills.

It helps you focus.

Mindfulness is best for people with ADHD mainly because it helps them focus. So, if constant daydreaming is keeping you from functioning well and completing your daily task, then you should start your meditation practice.

It helps you empathize with others.

It's no secret that people who practice mindfulness (like the Dalai Lama) are more compassionate and more emphatic than others are. A study conducted in 2008 shows that responders who practiced mindfulness meditation are more compassionate. This is because mindfulness promotes activity in the regions of the brain that are linked to empathy.

It keeps your mind young and vibrant.

A study conducted at Beth Israel Deaconess Medical Center shows that mindfulness meditation slows down the progression of age-related disorders such as dementia and Alzheimer's.

It improves your mental health.

Mindfulness helps people accept their painful emotions and experiences. It helps people gain perspective on maladaptive, self-defeating, and irrational thoughts. It helps ease a number of mental health issues, including substance abuse, depression, couple's conflicts, eating disorder, anxiety disorder, and obsessive-compulsive disorder.

Meditation also improves your mood. It helps build resilience and it keeps you from becoming overly emotional when exposed to challenging and stressful situations. To prove this, a study was conducted on Lama Oser, the Dalai Lama's right-hand man. He's been practicing meditation for more than 30 years. They scanned Lama Oser's brain using an MRI scanner and compared his results with over 100 different people. The results were astounding. Lama Oser's pre-frontal cortex activity ratio indicates high levels of well-being, equanimity, and resilience.

It improves creativity.

Divergent thinking and convergent thinking determines one's level of creativity. Divergent thinking allows you to come up with different ideas and convergent thinking helps you solidify those ideas into powerful concepts. A study conducted in Leiden university shows that mindfulness meditation significantly improves both convergent and divergent thinking.

It improves your overall health.

Studies show that mindfulness helps improve your physical health. It lowers down your blood pressure, it reduces chronic pain, it improves the function of your digestive system, and it also improves sleep.

It enhances your overall well-being.

Mindfulness helps you pay attention to the little things in life so it increases your life satisfaction. It helps you savor the little pleasures in life and help you deal with adversities and problems in a healthy way. It also increases your self-esteem and self-confidence.

Mindfulness also allows you to connect with others. It helps you improve your patience and tolerance, so it improves the quality of your relationships. It also reduces the feelings of loneliness and sadness.

It's free.

Most of the time, practicing mindfulness is free. So, this is a cost-effective way to fight stress, anxiety, and other mental diseases.

The regular practice of mindfulness can improve the quality of your life. It can improve the level of your happiness. It also improves your social skills and helps you connect with others in a more meaningful way. Mindfulness makes you feel more alive.

Frequently Asked Questions

If you're a beginner, a number of questions may come up in your mind. You may have doubts about meditation. You may wonder if mindfulness is the best stress reduction technique for you. Here are the answers to frequently asked questions about mindfulness practice:

Do I have to be spiritual to practice meditation?

No. It is a secular type of meditation and it is for everyone.

Do I have to enroll in a class?

It's better to enroll in the class, especially if you're serious with your mindfulness meditation practice. But, you can practice meditation by yourself. The tips and techniques contained in this book should be enough to help you jump start your mindfulness practice.

Can kids practice the mindfulness techniques, too?

Yes, absolutely! Kids can benefit from mindfulness meditation practice, too.

How long before I'll notice the results?

Mindfulness is a relaxation technique. So, you'll reap its stress-reduction benefits right away. However, it will take a while for you to reap the other benefits of mindfulness, such as improved cognitive function and physical health. The results of meditation are highly variable. This means that people who practice meditation may encounter different results. But, most people can already see the change in their life after a couple of weeks.

Do I have to sit down when I'm practicing mindfulness?

No. In this book, you'll find different techniques that will allow you to practice mindfulness in your daily life. You can practice mindfulness while you are doing your report or while brushing your teeth.

How can paying attention to simple activities like brushing my teeth help me?

Most of us go through life on an autopilot. Most of us walk from point A to point B without even noticing how we did it. We sometimes develop a habit or ruminating about the past or projecting about the future that we forget to focus on the present moment. Practicing mindfulness while you are doing simple activities like brushing your teeth will help you pay attention on the present moment. You begin to interact and process each experience as it is and this could create amazing changes in your life.

I do not have time to practice mindfulness meditation, what can I do?

It is best to set aside a few minutes of your time for this practice. But, if you're too busy, you can incorporate your meditation practice into your daily life. You can practice mindfulness while you are eating, while you are typing, or while you are working out. In this book, you'll learn the simple mindfulness practice that will allow you to practice mindfulness while performing your daily task.

Is mindfulness just a new age fad?

No, it's not a fad. It's something that you can practice for a couple of years and even for decades. Buddhist monks and spiritual mystics have practiced mindfulness for centuries.

Is mindfulness for me?

Mindfulness is for everyone; your age, status, race, location, or job does not matter. Everyone can benefit from it. It can improve your mental health and it can also help you cope with life. Mindfulness also helps make the most out of your potential.

Do I have to meditate every day?

Yes, especially if you want to reap the full benefits of mindfulness. Studies show that regular mindfulness meditation can help reshape your brain. Regular practice helps improve your cognitive function and it increases your emotional intelligence over time. It also improves your decision-making and people skills.

How long should I meditate?

You can start with three minutes a day during your first week of mindfulness practice. You could gradually increase your practice to 10 to 20 minutes. Then, after a few months of practice, you can increase your mindfulness meditation technique for

30 minutes to one hour; experiment and check what works well for you.

I am a restless person and I cannot sit still. Can I still practice mindfulness meditation?

Many people think that only those who have a calm and tranquil mind can practice mindfulness meditation, but the truth is that those who have restless minds can reap the most benefits from it. Mindfulness helps you pay attention to everything that you're experiencing, may it be physical pain, restlessness, emotions, or difficult feelings. Movement mindfulness is the best option for you if you have a restless mind. Also, it's a good idea to practice under the supervision of a meditation master. Your teacher can teach you specific techniques that address your specific needs.

Do I have to sit in a lotus position to do mindfulness meditation?

No, you can sit on a chair or a cushion in whatever position that's comfortable for you. You can even practice mindfulness meditation while standing up, moving, or lying down.

I have been struggling with mental health problems for years. Is mindfulness practice suitable for me?

Well, even though mindfulness is for everyone, people who have pre-existing mental health issues should only practice specific types of mindfulness meditation. If your mental health problem is relatively mild then you can simply practice the basic mindfulness meditation techniques for at least eight weeks. However, if you have serious mental health issues such as psychosis, anxiety, and depression, then you can talk to your therapist and try MBCT or mindfulness-based cognitive therapy.

Why do people practice mindfulness?

Different people practice mindfulness for different reasons. But here are the common reasons why people practice mindfulness:

Stress reduction

Depression

Insomnia or sleep disruption

Difficulty with concentration or focus

Anxiety

Chronic pain

Substance abuse recovery

The desire to live consciously and more fully

When you practice mindfulness, do you think about nothing?

No. Mindfulness does not and will not stop you from thinking. It simply allows you to notice your thoughts.

Can I practice mindfulness meditation alone or should I attend a class?

Yes, you can practice mindfulness meditation alone. You do not have to enroll in a class. But, if you have a restless mind or you are suffering from serious mental health issues, it's best to practice under the supervision of a teacher or a meditation master.

Is mindfulness the same with meditation?

Mindfulness is a type of meditation, just like other meditation techniques such as Kundalini meditation and Mantra meditation.

Tips for Beginners

Here are some of the tips that you can use to jumpstart your meditation practice:

Commit to it.

To reap the maximum benefits of mindfulness, you have to commit to it and practice regularly. You have to set aside a couple of hours of your day for your mindfulness. List it as part of your daily "to do" list and make sure that it's part of your daily schedule.

Start your day with mindfulness practice.

You can do your mindfulness practice anytime, but if you're a beginner, it's best to do this in the morning right after waking up or before leaving for work. This is because your mind is easier to tame in the morning before you begin your work and other daily activities. But, as you progress, you can start practicing mindfulness anytime you wish. You can practice while eating lunch or at night before sleeping.

Let go.

To live in the moment, you have to learn to let go of any distracting thoughts. This may be hard to do at first, but after weeks of mindfulness practice, this will become easier and more natural.

Learn to slow down.

In these modern times, people have to multi-task and do many things at the same time. But, to fully live in the moment, you must learn to slow down and calm your body and mind. When you talk to other people, try to pay attention to each word. When you're typing, pay attention to the sound of the keyboard as you hit each key.

Be patient.

Mindfulness practice is not easy. It will take you weeks, months, or even years to master it so you have to be patient with yourself and just keep going. But, as the days or weeks go by, you'll gradually experience positive changes in your life. You'll feel more relaxed and more alive.

Have fun.

A lot of people think that mindfulness practice is boring. This is not true. Mindfulness is the act of being present so it is actually fun and exciting. As mentioned earlier, living in the present moment is not as easy as most people think. So, you just have to enjoy the process. Once your mind is settled in, you'll reap the full benefits of mindfulness and you'll realize that your reality is even ten times better than your day dreams.

Do not give up.

If you have difficulty taming your thoughts or sitting still even for a couple of minutes, don't give up and immediately decide that mindfulness meditation is not right for you. The path to mindfulness is not an easy process. If you have a hard time sitting still, you're the type of person who needs mindfulness practice the most.

Mindfulness is an inexpensive way to improve the quality of your life. It improves your concentration and cognitive skills. It improves your work performance and most importantly, it increases the level of your happiness. Mindfulness is not an easy practice. To reap its full benefits, you need to be committed to it. You need to practice mindfulness regularly to master it, and once you do, you'll realize that it is worth all the effort.

Chapter 2: The Science Behind Mindfulness Meditation

If you are not persuaded by history, perhaps you will be more inclined to be persuaded by the science behind mindful meditation. In this day and age, we have the means to explore the minds of those who practice it on an ongoing basis and compare brain patterns and shapes to the patterns and shapes produced by those who do not practice mindfulness meditation. This may seem a little off the wall to some people, but bear in mind that scanners today can distinguish clearly the changes that take place in the brain during the process of aging. They can also see which areas of the brain are responsible for which actions or physiological purpose. That's quite spectacular, but when you back that up with medical science from the perspective of a medical expert like a brain surgeon, then you can't really argue the conclusions because even if the particular expert was skeptical about the link between calmness and mindfulness medication, it could be shown on a video that this same expert learned through practice that mindfulness meditation actually does make a difference to the way that you think.

Let's explore the scientific evidence for a moment so that you can see from a medical perspective the value of meditation and mindfulness. This may help you to decide whether you are prepared to use it to improve your life. Refer also to the chapter on health benefits, too, as this is relevant to your motivation when making your decision about whether you want to include mindfulness meditation into your life. There are different parts of the brain that are affected by meditation and mindfulness. A diagram of the brain may help you to picture it.

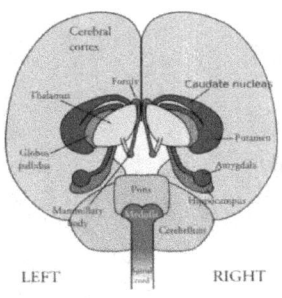

You can see quite clearly from this image the areas of the brain and although you may not be familiar with them, let's do a rundown on what they do and what they represent as this will help you to see how mindfulness meditation helps your mind to become more relaxed and able to see things in a clearer manner.

The areas of the brain that are affected by meditation are the Amygdala, and this is the sorting area for memories, deciding which memories are important and for the emotions and motivation that you feel during the course of your life. Your emotional responses are based here, which is why this area is so relevant to stress and anxiety, but it's also relevant to the clarity of thought, which is one of the areas in which mindfulness helps you considerably.

The thalamus sorts out sensory information, which means that when you touch, taste, or smell something, this part of the brain is recognizing the gesture and sending messages to other parts of the brain that are related to pleasure, discomfort, etc. Thus, Mindfulness affects this part of the brain since you are asked to be mindful of using your senses to enjoy your everyday life more. The scent of flowers or essential oils, the sight of something spectacular, and the sense of taste and touch are all part and parcel of the mindfulness experience.

The frontal lobe of the brain is where you find logic. This part of the brain has the power to help you to reason in a logical way and helps you to balance your emotions. The parietal lobe is affected during meditation, and this part of the brain is used for processing such things as language and mathematics as well as sensory experiences of other parts of the body.

You can see from this that the brain is complex, and the wiring that makes it work depends upon the function of each of the parts of the brain. Sarah Lazar did a wonderful video that explains the process that she went through when doubting the fact that meditation and mindfulness could help the development of parts of the brain. In her job as a Neuro Scientist at Harvard University, she worked on facts, and mindfulness seemed a little way out for her to really appreciate what was happening until she experienced it for herself and then tested the activity in the brains of people who meditated. Her findings were backed up by other scientific research, and what was found was that there were definite differences between the brain structure of those who meditated and those who did not. It's really worth watching her video on YouTube if you want to be persuaded because this is science at its best.

We know that the parietal lobe slows down during the meditative process, and this means that fewer messages are being processed by the brain, and there is less interference, thus enabling concentration and less interruption of the flow of thoughts. Sarah Lazar went through a period in her life when she was asked to stop the physical activity because of an injury. Her first approach toward getting better was to take up yoga, but this led her to discover mindfulness and meditation, which she was somewhat skeptical about. Bear in mind that she is a scientist, and thus, the approach that this was going to do her good was a huge question mark in her mind. Scientists work on proof, and this seemed a little too airy-fairy actually to believe. She could accept that stretching would help her mobility, but was uncomfortable with the claims of her instructor that compassion and other benefits could be gained from her yoga. In fact, she scoffed the idea of there being any kind of scientific proof that this was the case.

As she progressed with her experience, she started to notice differences in her approach to other people, and one of these differences was that she was indeed more patient and less judgmental and that she related to other people in a much more compassionate way. Thus surprised her because she hadn't expected it, and she thought it was simply a result that she had gained through the suggestion of her teacher, rather than being substantiated in any way. Her investigation into facts that she had gained showed her that there was indeed proof that meditation helped those with pain, for example, and that it lowered the level of stress. It improved the quality of life and in fact, made her more attentive to what was going on around her, and this was one of the facts that she had found out from her research, so it all made some kind of sense. However, being a scientist, she was impelled to investigate further because scientists don't just accept random facts, but want to know the physiological differences between people who meditate and those who do not. The overall conclusion she was able to make through studying was that people who performed meditation on a regular basis were happier in their lives and were content with themselves as opposed to those who did not. This sparked more curiosity.

A lot of what she found out was put down to neuroplasticity, which is an action that takes place in the brain when you perform an action on an ongoing basis, such as a habit. The communication between different areas of the brain is what keeps the brain active, and this was happening to people who meditate. MRI scans were used to detect the differences between people who, for example, could juggle and those who could not, and the differences were amazing. What does this have to do with meditation? The fact is that the shape of the brain and its ability to retain neuroplasticity depends upon the learning skills of the individual and the practices that that individual uses habitually.

Taking her investigations further, Doctor Lazar decided to try an experiment whereby she measured the brain activity of people who meditated on a regular basis against those who did not, and she was surprised that there were indeed differences. The grey matter in those who meditated was more prominent than in those who did not. They discovered using controls to measure against norms the area of the brain that dealt with memory and function and found that those who meditated had the same ability as 25-year-olds as opposed to being measured against others who did not meditate of their own age. This, of course, was a breakthrough. The study was questioned by others because there could have been other differences. For example, did the people in the study have different diets? However, following this, another study was done on people who had never meditated, and their MRI scans were compared to MRI scans of the same people after they had performed meditation for 30 to 4o minutes a day, and the results were pretty conclusive. There was more activity in the area of the hippocampus. Other areas that were affected were the temporoparietal junction, which is responsible for feelings such as compassion and the ability to understand and empathize. Another area that showed great results showed a decrease in activity, and this related to the fight or flight impulse of the brain to stimuli and meant that there was less liability to panic, and thus, the subjects were calmer. This area was the amygdala area of the brain. It was a pretty conclusive study that showed that mindfulness meditation could change the structure of the brain, and that may sound like a breakthrough, but it is backed up by an experiment that was done on the minds of Monks who practiced meditation on a regular basis. Doctor Lazar's findings can be found here.

Now let's look at the claim that the minds of monks showed different results to the average man in the street. In 1992, neuroscientists, Richard Davidson, took up the challenge and did scans of the brains of Buddhist monks, and these revealed interesting data. The Buddhist leader, the Dalai Lama, asked Davidson, "If you can use your modern tools to measure and study anxiety, fear, and depression, why can't you use them for studying compassion?" It wasn't a bad question to ask because the levels of compassion are indeed different when it comes to the minds of those who use it in a day-to-day manner. Davidson saw the merit of what the Dalai Lama was suggesting and found that people who are generous toward others and who are happier in their day to day lives suffered less stress, anxiety, and depression, so both ways gave him answers that he was looking for, but the approach of the Dalai Lama was intended to improve upon the attitude of mankind and the way in which he operates compassion — albeit from the experience of meditation on a regular basis.

Strangely enough, the immune response to the flu jab was noted in subjects who meditated on a regular basis. However, what Davidson noticed was the plasticity of the brain and the level of "bien d'etre" or wellbeing in the brains of those who meditated giving no doubt at all that meditation helped to keep the brain young and to experience less of the response that the area of the brain that deals with fight or flight usually has, meaning that people were calmer and more in control of their lives. This helps us to take huge steps toward understanding how the brain works and what meditation does to improve that work. One can conclude from the studies that have taken place over the years that meditation improves the function of the brain and thus is beneficial in cutting down episodes of anxiety, depression, and related ailments. In the fight against stress in the 21st century, it is a natural way to cope with stress long term rather than dealing with stress on a short-term basis as an illness by the use of traditional medications. I hope that this chapter is something that interests you because if you are in the slightest skeptical about the use of Mindfulness Meditation, you are in good company, and you will see from the experiences of scientists that Mindfulness Meditation has been proven to be effective on patients undergoing tests that show differences in the way that the brain responds to the stimuli of meditation. You will experience this change as well as a change in your demeanor over the course of practicing mindfulness meditation.

Chapter 3: Understanding Mindfulness

• Mindfulness is not as much about paying attention on the good things, as it is about not paying attention to the bad things. If there are ideas or thoughts that make you feel down and negative, it is important to keep in mind that you are not supposed to be focused on them.

• Mindfulness connects areas of the brain that deals with the cognitive functions and attention. The process involves paying attention to the details and not missing out on important things.

• There is growing evidence that mindfulness can alter the brain and the resulting triggers "the relaxation response" that can turn sets of genes on or off.

• Making mindfulness part of your life can be life changing and your health and general well-being will greatly benefit from it.

IMPACT OF MINDFULNESS

Avoid stress

When we are mindful of each and every moment, we are in control of our mind. This control allows us to avoid unnecessary stress and worry. We learn to take things as they come.

Better Productivity

Mindful people, on record show better productivity than people who keep focusing on their past or their future too much. Those who live in the present and enjoy it, win.

Better Health

Overall health gets the undivided attention it needs. When we live life worrying about everything, we ignore or neglect the things here and now. Mindfulness ensures that we pay more attention to our health.

Increases Mental Acuity

Mindfulness is not simply about awareness, it also includes observation. So when you are mindful, you are also being acutely observant of all the things around you. This increases mental acuity.

Helps with Coping

When we are mindful, we cope better with things. We become aware of what affects us and in what way. This leads us to avoid negativity and heal faster.

Mindfulness has been used in psychotherapy as a tool to deal with mental stress, tensions, anxiety and a whole host of other problems. The truth is, we are all running. Running towards something, running away from something! But we are running. This chase has led us to a stage where we do not take a moment to stop and think, "This moment is never going to come back!" We prepare for a future that is not promised and we think of a past which we cannot change. Instead, why not simply choose to live the present and be mindful of every moment.

HOW TO PRACTICE MINDFULNESS

Life can get busy with the fast pace of work, chores, errands and taking care of the kids. However, you can find time to practice mindfulness for more peace and joy in your life. People are concerned with the economy, worry about their finances, and their future. It sure can cause a lot of stress, which in turn can cause mood and physical changes.

Research shows that many people wish they could slow down and smell the roses more often. They feel rushed. They live life in the fast lane trying to accomplish their goals and do what they need to do, but when they get home at night and finish the tasks for the evening, they are beyond exhausted. Many experience burn out at one time or another. Many deal with anxiety and depressive disorders. Many simply feel like robots- experiencing little to no joy.

If you are feeling anything like what it has just been just described, here is a good news for you. Researchers have been studying the practice of mindfulness on stress, depression and are finding that it actually decreases negative symptoms and helps people to live happier, healthier lives. Mindfulness is growing rapidly around the world, as more and more people are experiencing remarkable changes as a result of this technique.

Practicing mindfulness is very simple. Just find a quiet place to sit down, take a few deep breaths, and relax every inch of your body. Your goal is to stay aware of your present moment and forget about the past or the future. As you breathe in and out, focus on your breath. As you breathe in, feel the air entering your lungs. As you exhale, focus on exhaling any negativity in you. As you keep your focus on your breathing, you will by default not be thinking about other things. If random thoughts come (as they will), simply acknowledge the thought and return your focus to your inhale and exhale.

Make time at your convenience every day to sit and practice mindfulness meditation. In the beginning weeks, try to do this for 15 to 20 minutes, but after that aim for 40 minutes a day. This may seem like a long time to sit still, but remember that as you are practicing mindfulness, you are combating stress, depression, anger, and all sorts of negative emotions that have been plaguing your mind for decades.

Do you know what you will find as you practice mindfulness? Your days will become brighter. You will find yourself being aware of your breathing throughout the days. You will be able to enjoy your present moments throughout the day much more. While you are sitting in traffic for an hour after work, instead of getting angry, you will be at ease, feeling more peaceful and joyful just for the fact that you are alive and breathing. You will find yourself being more present in your spouse and children's lives. You will engage with people more in a loving way. You will be more accepting, less judgmental; more connected with your spiritual self, more compassionate, and more emotionally stable.

Go ahead and begin your mindfulness journey today. Make a commitment to slow down and smell the roses. Begin with a few minutes here and there. Test it out. I think you will be very pleased with the results. After all, we all simply want to be full of love, peace, and joy, so if mindfulness is a ticket to that state, let us practice it!

Chapter 4: Mindfulness Meditation

The purpose of doing mindfulness meditation is to understand our feelings and sensations and focus more on what surrounds us in the moment. One has to choose a quiet place and the best sitting posture. They should then sit comfortably and listen to whatever goes through their mind, without reacting to it in any way.

The following tips can help you do meditation successfully:

Choose the best Location

This should be a quiet environment where nothing will interfere with you as you meditate. The location can be part of home or under a tree. It should be quiet and peaceful, and one should release himself/herself from their daily tasks.

This will help the individual create a space for helping them carry out their meditation. One may choose to keep beautiful flowers or some nice pictures on the table. You can also soften the light by lighting candles.

Stay comfortable

You will only meditate for a short period of time, and this calls for you to get comfortable. Maintain the room temperature at a level which is conducive for you. Since your body temperature may drop, ensure that you carry a blanket with you. Pillows and cushions can help you to sit comfortably. Your clothing should also be good as it should not interfere with you when meditating in any way. If it is too hot, do not wear heavy clothes, but if it is cold, ensure that that you wear warmer clothes.

Increase time gradually

Since you are a beginner to meditation, you cannot meditate for hours non-stop. Choose a short time, usually around 5-10 minutes should be enough for beginners. If you start with a longer time, you will be overwhelmed. Do it by incrementing the time in small intervals, and ensure that you do an improvement after each increment. Feel free to use a timer as this will help you know once an increment has elapsed. Distracting alarms should not be used as they may divert your attention from meditation.

Use different postures

Meditation can be done using a number of different postures. The best type of posture varies from each individual. It is advised that you choose the best posture for you by trying different ones out. This posture should be the one you feel most comfortable in. Instead of sitting, you can choose to lie down, or you can even walk while meditating. Try to use different postures, and alternate between these using cushions or pillows. Most beginners who try to lie down during meditation end up falling asleep, so it may be better to use this method later on down the line.

How to Maintain the Best Posture

The following are some of the things you should do so as to maintain a good and relaxing posture during meditation:

Take a seat- Choose the best seat for you, and this should be the one to make you comfortable. The seat can be a chair, a park bench or some meditation cushion. This should be coupled with a nice selection for the environment in which you will do your meditation.

Be keen on what the legs do- If you have not kept a cushion on the floor, just keep your legs at the front while crossing them. If you are good in maintaining a yoga posture while seated, this is the best time for you to do it. If you are seated on a chair or on a bench, ensure that you keep your feet touching the floor.

Straighten the upper body, but do not stiffen it- The spine should be kept in such a way that it will maintain its natural curvature. The head and the shoulders should be made to sit comfortably on top of the vertebrae.

Keep the upper arms parallel to the upper body- The arms should then be rested on top of your legs. Once you keep your upper arms by your sides, the hands will automatically fall into the right place. Do not keep them too back or too forward.

Drop the chin and gaze gently downward- At the same time, you should lower your eyelids. You may also choose to lower them completely, but you have to know that no one expects you to close your eyes completely during meditation. Even if something new comes before your eyes, just allow it to stay there and avoid diverting your attention to it.

Maintain the posture for few moments- Now that you have found the best posture for you, keep it for a few minutes' start meditating. Pay your attention to your body sensations and to your breathing. Take advantage of the best posture for your arms, legs and spine and begin meditation.

Begin again- If you have succeeded in maintaining your posture, just pay attention to your breathing, as your breathing in and as you breathing out. You will sometimes find your attention being diverted from all the thoughts racing through your head, and this is inevitable. Once it occurs to you, accept that is normal and everyone who does meditation goes through this. You should then try to do anything possible so you can return your attention back to the breathing. This calls for you to take a deep inhalation, hold it and then do a deep exhalation. Holding your breath will help you focus on how you feel on the inside. Focusing on the good feelings will help you overcome stress and any anxiety you are going through.

Choosing an Instructor

If you want to make meditation techniques to be a part of your daily life, it is recommended that you do it using a meditation instructor or teacher. These are everywhere, even online via video chats, and they will guide you on how to do it effectively. It is good for you to know how to meditate from someone, who is a trained professional, or at least has some sort of high level experience with meditation. This will ensure that you definitely succeed with meditation, and will ensure you overcome any stress or anxiety you may have in your life.

When choosing a meditation instructor, it is good for you to ask yourself the following questions:

Does the instructor have the qualities you need?

You must have pictured some of the qualities you expect the instructor to have back in your mind. Once you have identified an instructor, ask yourself whether they have those qualities. For you to learn something from him or her, you have to like them, and their qualities will determine whether you like them or not. If you like them, there is a possibility that you can establish a string of connections or a healthy relationship, this will be of great significance to you.

Is the instructor open and accessible?

The instructor should be relaxed, caring and compassionate. Also, the instructor has to be willing and ready to work according to your schedule, otherwise, he or she will not be the best instructor for you.

Does the instructor understand mindfulness meditation deeply?

The instructor should be well experienced in teaching people the practice of mindfulness meditation. If they are not experienced, ask them whether they are well trained. Experience and training go hand in hand so if you could get someone who has both that would be a perfect fit.

Are they friendly?

A good meditation instructor should be friendly. However, do not judge by their outward appearance and then conclude if they are friendly or not. It will be good if you interact with them on a regular basis before beginning the classes. The eye communication between you and the instructor should give you an indication if things will run smoothly or not. Choosing the best instructor is vital as you will have the opportunity to with them share what is stressing you. This can be quite a daunting task and it must be done without fear or feeling ashamed. Your instructor will help you as much as they can so they can help get you out of the current situation you are in.

Chapter 5: Preparation: Setting And Body Mechanics

The practice of meditation entails establishing a formal schedule specifically devoted to cultivating mindfulness. This is not an easy task. Developing mental habits require energy. This may seem quite counterproductive to the idea of meditation, which should be free flowing and natural. To address this, a bit of strategy is needed. Since the mind is like a cup of muddy water, allow a specific time to clarify it first. At the start of your meditation practice, give your mind enough time to settle down so you wind up with clear water. Do not do anything to force this settling as it should be a natural, spontaneous process. The very act of sitting down leads to mind settling.

Where to Sit

The condition of your surroundings affect your meditative practice. Choose a place that is quiet and uplifts you even if it only is a tiny corner of your apartment. It should be away from too much noise (though not necessarily sound-proof) and other stimuli, or a place where your emotions cannot easily be provoked. It may be helpful to sit in the same spot solely reserved for meditation. You will soon associate this place with the serenity of deep concentration, helping you reach deep states faster.

Certain traditional paraphernalia can help you set the proper mood. You can darken the room and light a candle or incense. You can also ring a little bell to signal the start and end of your sessions. They may be encouragement to some; however, they are by no means crucial to the meditation practice.

When to Sit

The Middle Ways, as a description of Buddhism, is considered as a rule in setting a time for your mindfulness meditation: Do not underdo it. Do not overdo it. Set up a practice schedule and stick to it. Remember that your schedule should feel like an encouragement and not a burden.

It is good to meditate in the morning when your mind is fresh, before getting yourself buried in your daily responsibilities. This tunes you up and lets you handle things throughout the day more efficiently. Take note that you should be completely awake. Wash your face or take a shower before starting. You may first do a bit of exercise to get your circulation flowing. Meditating in the evening is also fine. It is a great way to cleanse and rejuvenate your mind of all the burdens that have accumulated during the day. It also helps you sleep better.

For beginners, meditating once a day is enough. It is fine if you feel like you want to meditate more, just remember not to overdo it. Allot time to integrate meditation into your life, and let the practice grow gradually. Make it a steady and consistent effort. As you become more interested in meditation, you will find yourself making more room for it in your schedule. For some seasoned meditators, three to four hours of practice comes naturally without making any negative impact in their daily lives.

How to Sit

The Buddhist approach to meditation follows that body and mind should be connected. There is better energy flow throughout the body if it is positioned erectly. Bending the body changes the flow, which can directly interrupt your thought process. If you need a chair to do meditation, sit up straight with feet planted on the ground. If you prefer using a cushion such as a gomden or zafu, sit comfortably with legs crossed and your hands placed on your thighs palm-down. The hips should not be rotated forward nor tilted back. You must have a feeling of strength and stability. Your shoulders should be leveled as well as your hips. Your spine should be straight and aligned.

The first thing you must have is body awareness. You may prop yourself up on a chair and yet not be completely attuned to what your body is actually feeling. When starting a meditation session, spend some time settling into your posture. Feel how your spine is being drawn up from the top of your head in a way that your posture is lengthened. You can imagine placing your bones in the right order and your flesh hanging off that structure. This will help you feel relaxed and very much awake. Check and correct your posture at once if you find yourself getting hazy, dull, or falling asleep.

For strict mindfulness practice, open your eyes and gaze downwards, softly focusing two inches in front of your nose. This will make you purposefully ignore what is going on in the surroundings, reducing sensory input as much as possible.

How Long To Sit

Sit as long as you can, but, again, do not overdo it. Most beginners meditate for twenty or thirty minutes. It may initially be difficult to sit longer than this. Since the posture and mental skills are generally unfamiliar to Westerners, it will take some time for their body to adjust to them. As you become accustomed to the practice, you can extend your sessions gradually. It is recommended that after around one year of steady practice, you should be meditating comfortably for one hour per session.

As a general rule, determine the minimum length of time that is comfortable for you to practice then add five more minutes to it. There is, however, no strict rule as to the duration for sitting. There would be days when it will be physically impossible for you to sit longer (e.g. due to illness). This does not mean cancelling your meditation for the day though, as it is crucial to meditate regularly. Ten minutes of practice is already very beneficial.

Take note that you should decide the duration of your session before starting, and not while meditating. This will easily predispose you to restlessness. You can use a watch but you should not look at it every several minutes to see how you are doing. This completely kills your concentration, and agitation will set in. Do not peek at the clock until you think the whole meditation period has passed. Ideally, you do not even have to consult the clock at all, or at least not during every session.

Chapter 6: Meditations

In Chapter 2, we discussed basic mindfulness meditation as one of the techniques which can be used to practice mindfulness on a daily basis. Meditation is a mental training exercise which helps to discipline your mind into focused, present thinking. The practice revolves around the flow of breath through your body and the calming and centering effect that this brings.

Again, science backs up the value of meditation. During meditation, brain scans show increased activity in the areas that control pain tolerance, memory, self-awareness and goal setting as well as decreased activity in the areas responsible for anxiety and depression.

When scientists compared the brain activity of Buddhist monks to people who do not practice meditation, they found that the center in the brain associated with empathy is far more developed in the monks than in non-meditators. The monks also exhibited a higher rate of alpha brain waves which have been known to decrease the prevalence of negative moods and emotions. Studies have also shown that after eight weeks of meditating, the brain showed more dense matter in the areas associated with learning, memory and emotion and the amygdala, which we know deals with fear and anxiety, had decreased brain matter. Meditators have also been proven to have the ability to produce a greater number of antibodies to the flu virus than non-meditators.

Changes attributed to meditation can even be seen on a cellular level. Your cells have a protective protein complexes called telomeres which help reduce damage to DNA and decrease the rate of cell death. Reduced telomere length has been linked to diseases like cardiovascular disease, cancer and diabetes. When cancer survivors completed a meditation program their bodies showed a marked increase in telomere length. We are, of course, not espousing that meditation is a cure or preventative measure on its own for any serious disease, but it is another weapon in the armory that we can build along with general healthy living habits and a good diet (Salt, Brown & Moffat, 2015).

Breath Exercises

During meditation, there is a strong focus on breathing. Breathing is your body's way of transporting oxygen into your bloodstream. When your brain has a constant supply of oxygen rich blood, you are able to think more clearly and deal with stressful situations in healthier ways. One of the physical signs of anxiety and panic attacks is shortness of breath and hyperventilation. Hyperventilation is when your breathing quickens to such an extent that the balance of oxygen intake and carbon dioxide expulsion is disturbed.

If we have disturbed breathing, it has an enormous impact on our body. We start to feel light-headed and we cannot think clearly. Our legs become weak and we are forced to sit or lie down. Being unable to breathe properly instils a deep sense of panic within us because this is a very basic requirement for survival.

There are a few breathing techniques which can be used in order to help alleviate anxiety.

- **Exhale for longer:** This may sound counter-intuitive, as the idea of taking deep breaths is always what accompanies breathing to calm ourselves, but in reality, exhaling correctly is just as important as inhaling correctly. The act of inhaling is linked to our sympathetic nervous system, which is responsible for our flight or fight response. The act of exhaling is linked to our parasympathetic nervous system, which is responsible for helping us to relax and calm down.

This breathing technique, therefore, involves ensuring that you exhale for longer than you inhale. If you are inhaling for four seconds, then exhaling for six seconds, you will ensure that you do not hyperventilate and cause a build-up of carbon dioxide in your bloodstream.

- **Breathe from your diaphragm:** Your diaphragm is a triangular-shaped muscle that is located just below your lungs. By learning to use your diaphragm to breathe, you can actually expend less energy. The easiest way to train yourself to breathe from your diaphragm is to sit in a chair or lay with your head and knees propped up by pillows. Then place one hand on your belly, just below your rib cage and the other over your heart. Inhale and exhale deeply through your nose only, as you normally would at first, and notice whether your chest or your belly rises and falls. The key is to practice so that your belly is moving when you breathe and not your chest. This will take some practice and will be tiring at first but when you are naturally breathing from your diaphragm without effort, you will be expending less energy to breathe.

- **Breathe in calmness, breathe out stress:** Close your eyes and take in a few big, deep breaths. Imagine that the air you are breathing in contains only peace and calm. When you breathe out, imagine that you are expelling stress and anxiety from your body. Visualization is key here. It doesn't matter how you picture the calm inhalation or exhalation of stress, but the images must be vivid enough to really allow your body to feel a sense of peace entering and stress exiting.

- **Progressively relax your muscles through breathing:** In this technique, the goal is to relax all the muscle groups in your body. Lie flat on your back, preferably on the floor. With each intake of breath, tense a group of muscles, on the exhale, relax that group of muscles. Starting with the muscles in your feet, inhale and tense your feet muscles then exhale and relax those muscles. Each act of tensing and relaxing must be done consciously and with the focus only on those muscles. Work your way up your entire body with this process until you have relaxed every voluntary group of muscles in your body (Ambardekar, 2018).

Meditating with Nature

Nature is most certainly the easiest place to practice mindfulness. When we physically take our bodies and minds to a place where the troubles and concerns of daily life are literally left behind, we cannot help but be present in the moment. Such a place could be a mountain or national park, but it could also be as accessible as a park in the suburbs or even sitting in your own lounge surrounded by potted plants if that is the closest to nature that you are able to get.

Be Mindful First

Before attempting to meditate in nature, we must ensure that we are practicing mindfulness there first. As you enter the place you have chosen, start to ensure that you are focusing yourself only on that place and your time in it. This is not the time to concern yourself with the traffic you experienced on the way there nor the dinner party you have to attend later on. Those things belong to the past and the future and they have no bearing on your place in nature at that moment.

If you are with others, try to discuss beforehand the expectations that each has of the other for the trip. Try to only go with people that will respect your wish for quiet and a mindful state of mind. If you know that a friend is experiencing a difficult time, go into the experience with the understanding that the excursion may not be an experience of quiet and solitude. If you are going on an excursion into nature for the specific purpose of practicing mindful meditation, then it is best not to take people with who will be unable to respect that your desire to be mindful, for whatever reason.

The Act of Meditation

When you are in a state of mindfulness, you can commence a meditative session when you feel comfortable. If you are well-versed in meditation, you may slip easily into a state of relaxation. If you are a beginner, you can start by closing your eyes and trying some of the breathing methods we discussed earlier. Remember not to attempt to force away intrusive thoughts or feelings. Acknowledge these thoughts and feelings without judgement and release them. See them as clouds drifting in and your mindful focus as a wind blowing the clouds away.

Meditating by Using Your Senses

Once you have managed to attain a general feeling of relaxation, you can start to open up your senses and meditate on each. Focus on your hearing. Listen to the various sounds that make up the chorus of nature. Try to identify each individual sound and then notice how each sound comes together to form the soundtrack of the place you are in.

Use your sense of touch to pull your hands through soil. Feel each grain and lump and acknowledge the temperature of the soil.

Touch nearby plants, gently run your finger along the leaves and experience the tiny follicles on each. What can you smell? Take in the earthiness of the soil and the scent of a flower.

When you have used all of your senses to individually experience the elements of the place you are in, you can quietly look around you and marvel at how each of these things fits perfectly into your surroundings. Consider your relationship to all of the things around you (Coleman, 2017).

Meditating Before Leaving Home

Our homes should be places of peace and harmony. In our homes, we can be ourselves, without being flustered and concerned with the problems of the outside world. We inevitably need to leave these sanctums though, and it is important that we are properly prepared when we do to avoid being bombarded and dragged down by any negativity we may encounter during our day. One way to prepare ourselves is by meditating to ensure that we are centered.

If you work outside the home and have a family, the best time to meditate is going to be before your family wakes up and the hustle and bustle of the morning begins. Set your alarm clock for just ten minutes earlier than you normally would. You can even meditate in your bed before you get up or on the floor of your bedroom.

If you struggle to get into a meditative state there are helpful apps on your cell phone that can guide you through a meditation, just pop your earphones in and invest in yourself with ten minutes of centering and breath focus. If you are lucky enough to have a garden, this is an excellent place for at-home meditation.

Meditation can be a family affair too, as long as everyone is on the same page. If you can get your partner and children to meditate at the same time as you, that's even better because not only are you heading out into the world with your energy shield on but so is your whole family. You are also less likely to have early morning squabbles, which can put a serious damper on our day if the whole family is in the same mindset.

Encouraging your children to meditate before school is an excellent way for them to get into the concentration zone for school and shield them from the raucous energies that are often present on most playgrounds.

Chapter 7: Mindfulness In Everyday Life

You may remember being told as a child to be mindful of your manners. The problem is that people have this idea that mindful behavior is stifling in some way. However, nothing could be further from the truth. It is actually liberating. Let's show you some ways in which you can use mindfulness in your everyday life to improve your health and improve your state of mind.

Meals and drinks

You may think that it doesn't matter that you eat your meals on the go and don't choose things that are particularly nourishing. The fact is that you do need to get back to concentrating on what you eat and taking more time eating it. The digestive system in the human body suffers a lot through human neglect and this also plays out when it comes to stress and to other ailments. If your digestive system is sluggish it affects so many areas in your life. Thus, you need to practice mindfulness when you eat. That might sound a little convoluted, but it isn't. You will see a difference after you have done this for around a week, so give it a chance.

As you prepare your food, use your sense of smell to enjoy and savor what you are making. It doesn't mean you have to make a big deal of it, but you do need to allow your senses to play out the roles that you have been avoiding. Smell your coffee. Smell your food and let that give you a sense of anticipation about what you are about to eat. Then, when it slides onto your tongue, be aware of the differences in the textures and the tastes and chew your food sufficiently to help your digestion. When Lily worked for an advertising company, she never gave herself time to eat at lunch. She was too busy trying to impress her boss. Instead of eating sensibly, she started to gulp down her food and was very surprised by the illnesses that followed, though she shouldn't have been surprised at all. When you don't take any notice of what you are eating and you are even guilty sometimes of swallowing before you have chewed your food, it's little wonder that the gut complains.

In a similar way, you need to make your food look inviting so that you can see and look forward to what you prepare for yourself. If you can't do this in your office environment, take your own lunch, so that you are not tempted to opt for bad choices. Mindfulness when eating includes enjoying the touch of the fruits that you eat, enjoying the aromas, the tastes and the textures and also being aware of that moment when you are actually eating, rather than considering this unimportant. It's vitally important to your health and will also allow you to cut down your stress levels. Do you find yourself sluggish in the afternoons? It's probably because you have undigested food in your stomach and have eaten it too quickly. You also need to enjoy the taste of water. If you fuel your body with the right foods and drink plenty of water, it makes a whole heap of difference to the way that your body feels. If you don't like water, challenge yourself to flavor it with fruit.

Mindful observation

Sometimes when you cannot find answers to the problems that life throws at you, you just need to distance yourself from those problems for answers to come. People work too hard at finding solutions when the mind simply needs to be inspired. Mindfulness helps you to do this. Mindful observation is a wonderful thing to do if you are looking for a little space in your day and a bit of inspiration. Place a piece of something natural on the table in front of you and concentrate on it. Try not to be distracted from it. You are looking at this object as if it's something you have never seen before. Notice its construction, follow the contour lines and the patterns that nature has created. You don't have to think anything.

You simply observe whatever it is that you chose to observe and try to cut out all other thoughts. The fact is that mindfulness works best when you are not thinking about it and that's where a lot of people go wrong. Simply close of your mind to thoughts and observe because it helps you to see a side to life that you may have been taking for granted. This can help you to find answers in your life. Sometimes you are throwing so many questions at your mind that the mind cannot process it all let alone giving you answers. When you use mindful observation, you free your mind of that feeling of being imprisoned and begin to observe without any kind of conscious interference. Nature is inspirational. Let it inspire you.

Chapter 8: Concept Of Mindfulness

Proverbs 4:23; Keep your heart with all vigilance, for from it flow the springs of life.

•Mindfulness means keeping up a moment-by-moment awareness of our thoughts, feelings, bodily sensations, and surrounding environment, through a delicate, gentle touch.

Mindfulness likewise includes acknowledgment, implying that we focus on our thoughts and emotions without judging them; without accepting, for example, that there's a "right" or "wrong" approach to think or feel in a given minute. At the point when we practice mindfulness, our contemplations tune into what we're detecting right now instead of reiterating the past or envisioning what's to come.

Despite the fact that it has its underlying foundations in Buddhist reflection, a common act of mindfulness has entered the American standard as of a later period, to a limited extent through the work of Jon Kabat-Zinn and his Mindfulness-Based Stress Reduction (MBSR) program, which he propelled at the University of Massachusetts Medical School in 1979. Since that time, a huge number of studies have reported the physical and mental well-being advantages of mindfulness generally and MBSR specifically, motivating incalculable projects to adjust the MBSR model for schools, hospitals, prisons, veterans centers and beyond.

1 Mindfulness is frequently referred to as an awareness discipline. It is a method for training the mind, heart, and body to be completely present with life. Albeit and regularly connected with meditation, mindfulness is considerably more than a meditation strategy. Mindfulness is in a general sense a method for being; a method for inhabiting our bodies, our mind, and our moment-by-moment involvement with transparency and receptivity. It is a profound awareness; a

knowing and encountering of life as it emerges and passes away in every minute.

As indicated by Shapiro and Carlson (2009), mindfulness can be defined as "the awareness that emerges through deliberately attending in an open, kind and observing way." Mindfulness can be comprehended as both an inherent and ever-present mindfulness (mindful awareness), and a progression of explicit practices intended to enhance mindful attention and awareness (mindful practice).

A Christ-like perspective implies that you live in the present moment by just concentrating on each thing in turn as opposed to hauling stuff from the past or stumbling on what's to come. This can only be accomplished through a renewing of the mind as Paul prompts in Romans 12:2 (And be not conformed to this world: but be ye transformed by the renewing of your mind, that ye may prove what is that good, and acceptable, and perfect, will of God.) And put our focus on heavenly things as exhorted in Colossians 3:2 (Set your affection on things above, not on things on the earth). The modern world is tied in with performing multiple tasks and accomplishing such a large number of things at once, to lament losing any of it and to consistently need more. This isn't what humans need to do as the book of scriptures says that you need to not conform with the world, however to renew the mind. This is the quintessence of mindfulness, which will prompt a real existence not guided by feelings over what others may think, or the need to have more than others or be impeccable, yet rather to look upon Christ.

Jesus was one of the most mindful people to ever lived. He was constantly receptive to what was happening around him and reacted to that reality. He would perceive the aimlessness of the individuals gathering around him, their yearning, and even the progression of power from his body when he was touched by the hemorrhaging lady. Much the same as

Jesus, careful individuals are more in line with reality that they realize how to respond in a wide range of situations and realities.

Jesus was mindful and resolute in his motivation which gave him significant serenity. All he was ever worried about was God's exemplary nature and the Kingdom of God. By individuals being much the same as Jesus in concentrating on their motivation and purpose, they can shut out stress, uneasiness, and be available to what's going on in their individual lives. As it says in Hebrews 10:22-23 (Let us draw near with a true heart in full assurance of faith, having our hearts sprinkled from an evil conscience, and our bodies washed with pure water. Let us hold fast the profession of our faith without wavering; (for he is faithful that promised;), we have to hold on to our faith without faltering, given that God in paradise is dedicated to satisfy what he has guaranteed. By believing that our future has been dealt with by our confidence in Christ, we can be progressively mindful in living right now.

Mindfulness is the ability to know what's happening in your head at any given moment, without getting carried away by it. Imagine how incredibly useful this could be in your daily life. Being mindful is about learning to respond intelligently, rather than react blindly. This practice can boost your health, happiness, and relationships. In fact, practising mindfulness is one of the simplest things you can do for your wellbeing.

Three Core Elements of Mindfulness

Mindfulness includes three center components: intention, attention, and attitudes (Shapiro and Carlson, 2009). Intentions includes knowing why we are doing what we are doing: our definitive point, our vision, and our yearning. Attention includes attending completely to the present moment as opposed to enabling ourselves to end up distracted with the past or future. Attitude, or how we focus, empowers us to remain open, kind, and inquisitive. These three components are not separate—they are interlaced, each advising and supporting the others. Mindfulness is this moment-to-moment procedure.

Intention

The main center part of mindfulness is intention. Intention is essentially knowing why we are doing what we are doing. At the point when we have recognized our intentions and can interface with them, our intention help propel us, helping us to remember what is genuinely significant. Perceiving our intentions includes inquiring into our most profound expectations, wants, and yearnings. Mindful attention regarding our own intentions causes us to start to carry oblivious qualities to awareness and choose whether they are extremely the qualities we need to seek after. The intention, with regards to mindfulness, isn't equivalent to (and does exclude) endeavouring or grasping for specific results or objectives. Or maybe, as a meditation instructor and psychotherapist Jack Kornfield puts it, "Intention is a direction, not a destination" (2009).

Attention

The second crucial part of mindfulness is attention. Mindfulness is tied in with seeing clearly, and in the event that we need to see plainly, we should be able to pay attention to what is here, presently, right now. Paying attention includes watching and encountering our moment-to-moment experience. But, this isn't so easy. Current research shows that our mind meanders roughly 47% of the time (Killingsworth and Gilbert, 2010). The human mind is regularly alluded to as a "monkey mind," swinging from thought to thought like a monkey swings from limb to limb. Mindfulness is an instrument that helps us tame and train the brain with the intention that attention winds up steady and centred, in spite of our mind's tendency to meander. Accordingly, attention is the part of mindfulness that encourages an engaged and clear observing of what emerges in our field of experience.

Frequently, as we attempt to pay attention, our attention winds are tense and contracted. This is on the grounds that we erroneously think we must be pushed or be watchful to focus our attention in a thorough manner. Notwithstanding, the meditation customs show us an alternate sort of attention, a "relaxed alertness" that includes lucidity and exactness without stress or vigilance(Wallace, 2006). This casual alertness is the sort of attention that is basic to mindfulness. Mindful attention is additionally profound and infiltrating; as Bhiku Bodhi notes "…whereas a mind without mindfulness 'floats' on the surface of its object the way a gourd floats on water, mindfulness sinks into its object the way a stone placed on the surface of water sinks to the bottom" (Wallace, 2006).

Attitude

Attitude, how we pay attention, is fundamental to mindfulness. For instance, attention can have a cool, basic quality, or a kind, inquisitive, and empathetic quality. Attending without bringing the attitudinal characteristics of interest, transparency, acknowledgement, and generosity into the training may bring about the attention that is censuring or shaming of inner (or outer) experience. This may well have outcomes in spite of the expectations of the training; for instance, we may wind up developing examples of analysis and endeavouring rather than serenity, transparency, and acknowledgement.

These attributes of mindfulness don't modify our experience yet basically contain it. For instance, if while we are rehearsing mindfulness, impatience emerges, we note the impatience with acknowledgement and kindness. We don't endeavour to substitute these characteristics for the impatience or use them to cause the impatience to vanish. The attitudes are not endeavours to cause things to be in a certain way, yet an endeavour to identify with whatever is with a particular intention in mind. By purposefully carrying the attention of mindfulness to our awareness with our own experience, we give up the habit for taking a stab at wonderful encounters, or of pushing aversive encounters away. Rather, we attend to and welcome anything that is here.

It might be valuable to consider mindfulness as a presence of heart just as mind. Indeed, the Japanese kanji for mindfulness is made out of two symbols, the top meaning presence and the base interpreted as "heart" or "mind." Mindfulness includes bringing heartfulness to every minute—carrying our full aliveness and care to the majority of our encounters.

Chapter 9: Why Practice Mindfulness?

The thing with mindfulness is that some of the most popular opinions regarding it are completely wrong. People put too much flair to it or have expectations that are absurd or unrealistic. Mindfulness is not supposed to fix you magically... for example, if you have depression, mindfulness will certainly help you become more peaceful. But you also need to take the necessary steps to deal with depression.

Here are five things that far too many people get wrong about mindfulness:

Mindfulness is not about "fixing you."

Mindfulness has never been about stopping one's thoughts

Mindfulness belongs to no religion.

Mindfulness is not meant to help you escape from reality

Mindfulness is no panacea

With all this in mind, why practice mindfulness? There are numerous reasons why you should practice mindfulness on the regular, as mentioned in the previous chapter. Mindfulness has been proven to improve lives as well as boost, among other aspects of health, and one's mental health.

Here are the top reasons why you should subscribe to the practice of mindfulness:

1: Mindfulness alleviates stress or at the very least some of it

We presently live in a "generation of stress." There is a lot of pressure on people today, and this often leads to a lot of accumulated stress. Stress will usually lead to health problems. At the very least, your mental health will suffer. Mindfulness is a great stress-prevention tool. People who practice mindfulness admit to feeling less stressed as they handle the issues that life serves them.

2: Mindfulness is more than just reducing stress levels

Certainly, stress reduction comes with mindfulness. However, the ultimate goal is not to reduce stress. The ultimate goal of mindfulness is to trigger the motion of our inner mental, emotional, and physical states. The goal is to make you more alive and more functional "in the present."

3: Mindfulness trains your body to thrive

You need to look no further than professional athletes for proof of this. Many pro athletes use mindfulness meditation to encourage peak performance. Collegiate basketball players are being coached to accept negative thoughts meditatively and transmute them into positive ones. Cycling champions have been coached to follow their breath for decades now. Big wave surfers are encouraged to brood on and transform their fears.

Sports psychologists have described these mindful techniques as being vital in the "coaching of the whole person." Once your mind is set right by mindfulness, it follows that your body will also be primed to perform at its best.

4: Mindfulness boosts creativity

Whether your art of choice is coloring, drawing writing, music, Etc., all of them have meditative practices that accompany them. The more 'present' you are, the more free your mind is and this can allow for more creative juices to flow.

5: Mindfulness strengthens your neural connections

By training your brain in mindfulness, you can build new neural pathways as well as networks in your brain, which helps you boost concentration, awareness, flexibility, and many other cognitive abilities.

6: Mindfulness reduces over-thinking and rumination

Often, what underlies anxiety is the unsavory duo of rumination and over-thinking. Once you worry about something, the brain is designed to commit to clinging onto the thing. It is very easy to be caught in a loop that has you replay every bad outcome that is possible, and this is not beneficial at all. Mindfulness helps you cease the endless worry and instead focus on the present.

7: Mindfulness boosts memory, focus, and performance

Being able to pay attention and focus on tasks at hand has to be one of the most vital cognitive abilities a human being can have. Seeing as mindfulness helps prevent mind-wandering and cluttering, it also helps you stay in the moment. You can give your undivided attention to the issues at hand. You are better able to focus on and solve problems competently.

8: Mindfulness helps greatly with emotional reactivity

Mindfulness helps you stay in the present. It makes you a "now" person. One perk that stems from this is that you are less emotionally reactive. You feel less compelled to recoil emotionally at every other thing that prods at you. You are better able to roll with the punches and only respond to those things that warrant it.

9: Mindfulness upholds cognitive flexibility

A **study** suggests that the practice of mindfulness not only helps you become less emotionally reactive; it also adds to your cognitive flexibility. If you observe most people that practice mindfulness (especially those who are great proponents of meditation as a tool to hone their mindfulness), you may notice that they are also great at self-observation that promptly disengages those pathways that were forged in the brain from prior incidences of learning; thus allowing incoming information to be understood in new, innovative ways.

10: Improves your general emotional health

By focusing on the present and affirming to yourself that indeed, you are valuable and effective in the present moment, you improve your self-image. You can adopt a more positive outlook on life. Two studies conducted on mindfulness meditation recorded decreased depression in more than 4,600 adults.

A study followed some 18 volunteer adults as they practiced mindfulness meditation for three years. This study unearthed that depression decreased and that these cases of reduced depression were long term in nature.

Further, cytokines, which are inflammatory chemicals that are released in response to stress may affect your mood and eventually lead to depression. A **review of multiple studies** suggested that mindfulness meditation could reduce depression by decreasing these chemicals.

11: Reduction in Age-related memory loss

Improvements in focus and attention, as well as clarity of thought, may play a major role in keeping your mind young. And when your mind is young, your body tends to stay young as well.

Kirtan Kriya is a mindfulness meditation technique which combines a chant or mantra with repetitive finger motions in a bid to focus your thoughts. In numerous cases of age-based memory loss, this technique helped improve participants' ability to do memory retention tasks.

What is more, a review of 12 studies discovered that multiple styles of mindfulness meditation **elevated attention, speed of thought, and comprehension** in older volunteer adults.

12: Mindfulness enables you to fight addictions better

The mental discipline and resolve that you develop through mindfulness meditation may help you deal with dependencies better. By practicing mindfulness, you are better equipped to face them head-on and break them. Your superior self-control and awareness will help you cut out addictions easier.

Research has shown that mindfulness meditation may help you learn to redirect your attention as well as boost your willpower. You will be in a better position to control your emotions as well as your impulses. Through time, you will be able to increase your understanding of the causes behind your most addictive behaviors.

One study which taught 19 recovering alcoholics meditation techniques showed that the participants who took in training and tried to apply it responded far better to their cravings compared to those that did not.

13: Mindfulness can help you handle pain better

Your perception of pain is connected to your mental state. In stressful conditions, it may be elevated.

For instance, a study used functional MRI techs in a bid to observe the activity of the brain as the participants experienced pain. Some of the participants had undergone as many as four days of mindfulness meditation training. The others had no meditation training.

The patients that had meditation training **showed increased activity in the brain centers responsible for pain-control**. They also reported less pain sensitivity.

With those amazing benefits you stand to benefit by practicing mindfulness, let us now learn how actually to practice mindfulness so that you know what to do to enjoy the amazing benefits this practice has to offer.

Chapter 10: Mindfulness Technique #1:

The Camera

Of the easiest ways to achieve mindfulness is to simply visualize or assume that there is an internal camera working in your mind. We actually have this internal camera. When you look at the world around you, you end up taking up only a fraction of the things that you actually become aware of through your senses. This is not an accident.

Based on our mental habits, our upbringing, and our past experiences we tend to focus more on certain things than others. There's really no right or wrong way to visualize the world except of course if it leads to negative results.

For example, if you tend to always pick on the negative then this leads to you being a negative person who always assumes the worst in people and situations. This is harmful. I just need you to step back and look at the process.

You see, whenever you're thinking there's always an internal camera. There's always a part of yourself that is somewhat detached from a particular situation. You can realize this most clearly when you think about a memory.

When you play back in your mind a memory, how does it feel? If you're like most people, it would feel like you're watching a video play out and you obviously took that footage with a camera. The camera is your internal camera. I need you to be conscious of your internal camera because you can be more mindful by learning how to maneuver this camera.

Two angles

Your internal camera has two angles depending on your habits. Some people have an internal camera that views the outside world from an internal angle. In other words, their memories show footage of them recording the outside world from a camera fixed within their eyes. When you watch the video footage, you see the world recorded from the perspective of the person that recorded that footage. It comes from the inside out.

Other people, on the other hand, take their mental video footage from the outside in. It's as if they have this floating camera outside and they can see themselves interact and move around a particular setting. Indeed, this is like watching a typical movie.

When you're watching a movie, you will see the actors on the screen. If you have an "outside in" camera angle, you watch yourself interact with your outside world in your memory.

Be aware of your internal camera and be awake on a moment-by-moment basis

Now that you acknowledge that you have an internal mental camera, the next step is to simply just let the camera operate by just letting it take footage. But what's important is that you are aware that this is happening. You're also watching screen after screen.

What's important here is that you don't get fully involved and emotionally worked up by the footage that your internal camera is taking. Instead, you just acknowledge that this is happening. This is the big difference between being aware of something and judging it. This is a crucial distinction.

Awareness versus judgment

Effective mindfulness is all about simply being aware. You just need to focus on awareness. Understand that your camera is panning back and forth, shifting gears, and looking at many different angles, but you shouldn't get thrown off by the images it collects.

You're not getting all emotionally worked up when certain mental images come to mind. This is your preferred mental state. This is how you should be doing it. You're practicing mindfulness correctly if you do things this way. You're just acknowledging things. Compare this with how most people normally look at memories and mental images.

Normally, people would see an image flash in their mind's eye and they get all worked up. Maybe it's an image of an ex-boyfriend or girlfriend. Maybe it's an image of a place that they have a negative association with. Whatever the case may be, when a certain image comes or when they are observing something with their mind's eye, they are drawn to negative states. This is judgment.

You need to learn that your camera is emotionally neutral. You don't have to get into a negative emotional state. You don't have to get thrown off. You don't have to get all upset. You just need to let the camera pan from picture to picture or image to image, from one angle to the next. Just let it do its thing.

Your job is to simply be aware that these images are coming to mind and to hold back from judging them. When you judge, you put a tremendous amount of pressure on yourself. When you judge, you get stressed out.

By constantly training yourself to view the world around you as well as your memories with your internal camera without judging, you increase the amount of relaxation and inner peace you get. This of course will not happen overnight.

There are certain images that instinctively freak you out. I completely get this. You're not alone, but you need to train yourself using daily mindfulness techniques to step away from judgment. The more you do this, the more at peace you will become. You will eventually reach a stage where it's very difficult for you to get thrown off and become upset

Chapter 11: Understanding Mindfulness

When I first came across the term 'mindfulness', I believed that mindfulness must be something extremely complex. However, when I looked at it, I realized that it isn't as complicated as it sounds. Let me explain what mindfulness truly is.

What Is Mindfulness?

Mindfulness means, "Living in the moment nonjudgmentally and peacefully."

When I say, "living in the moment", it means you are aware of your moment-by-moment feelings, thoughts, bodily sensations and surroundings. It also means that you should not judge your thoughts and feelings and accept them as they come without labeling them as "good" or "bad".

Today's life is fast-paced where you do things in a rush in order to move on to the next thing on your list. While doing things in a rush, you forget to live in the moment;

either you linger in the past or think about the future. When you stay concerned about the past or the future, you feel stressed out because you either cry over things that have already happened or become stressed about the many different hurdles that you may face in future.

To understand this better, think of the last time you ironed your clothes. Do you recall the process at all? I am sure you don't. Why? Simply because you were focused on doing that task quickly so you could do whatever was next on your list. Such urgency in your behavior restricts you from living in the present. You feel stressed out by thinking of the moment that is about to happen. While you ironed your clothes, you constantly worried about your next chore, which not only made you less attentive to the task at hand, but also increased your routine stress.

Whenever you don't pay attention to the moment, you miss out on the joy which the present offers you. Instead, you think about the unpleasant experiences of your life or the uncertainties of the future and become more anxious than ever. When you continue staying stressed and anxious for long, you fall in the depression trap and live a miserable life.

Mindfulness, on the other hand offers you the chance to be present in each moment as it occurs and enjoy it fully. When you stay focused in the moment at hand, you live it completely and enjoy its essence. This is how it reduces stress and anxiety. Let me further elaborate it in the next chapter.

How Mindfulness Affects Stress and Anxiety

A study published at Spanish Journal of Psychology proves that mindfulness reduces stress levels. When you try to live in the present, you don't let negative thoughts wander in your mind, which makes you feel less stressed than before.

Let me elaborate on how mindfulness positively affects your quality of life, and reduces stress, anxiety and depression.

How Does Mindfulness Helps You Reduce Stress?

To understand how mindfulness helps manage stress, recall a bad day at work when your boss yelled at you for not doing your work well. You returned home from work and started doing your routine chores like doing laundry or eating dinner with your family. Although you had left your workplace, your mind remained stuck in that moment, thinking of how that awful moment ruined your entire day. No matter what you did, you kept thinking of that unpleasant experience.

You know why that happened. It happened because you were forgetful of your present. Now let's see this situation from another angle.

Instead of being forgetful, you are mindful this time. You live each moment as it passes. Now, you are at home eating dinner with your family after returning home from a bad day at work. The feeling of humiliation strikes your mind as you remember the unpleasant experience at the office.

The first thing you do is be aware of your surroundings. You notice that you are having dinner with your family. You enjoy the discussion going on at the table. You let that thought pass by without being judgmental and cherish the moment you are currently having with your family. After a moment, the feeling of humiliation is gone.

That's how mindfulness reduces stress and brings peace in your life. It simply shifts your focus from the past or future to the present so you enjoy and cherish it and slowly forget all that has been bothering you.

When you become mindful, you live in the present, you don't allow your thoughts and feelings to linger in the past or panic about the future. Living in the moment helps you become aware of your thoughts and feelings. Whenever a negative thought crosses your mind, you pull your conscious mind back in the moment. As a result, you stop being judgmental of your thoughts and wandering off in thought, and start to live in the moment.

Now that you know what mindfulness is and how it helps you to manage stress, let me discuss some of the techniques, which you can implement to practice it.

Mindfulness Meditation

Mindfulness meditation is a research based western technique of meditation derived from an old Buddhist technique for meditation called Vipassana. The purpose of mindfulness meditation is to develop the skill of accepting our thoughts and feelings as they come without judging them. Furthermore, this technique was designed to improve the skill of paying attention to our thoughts and to accept them patiently.

In the US, 250 institutes have carried out over 1500 studies over the past few decades. All these studies suggested that Mindfulness Meditation is clinically effective in reducing stress, anxiety, and obsessive thinking.

In fact, a survey conducted by UMass Medical School's Center for Mindfulness Stress Reduction Program showed that Mindfulness Meditation reduced stress and anxiety levels by 40% in 15,000 patients.

In a nutshell, mindfulness meditation reduces stress and anxiety by making you more aware of your thoughts as they come. It cultivates patience in your consciousness as you stop judging your thoughts and feelings. That having been said, you must be wondering how you can practice mindfulness meditation. Let get into that now.

How to Perform Mindfulness Meditation

Here's how you can practice mindfulness-based meditation.

Choose a Peaceful Environment

To perform mindfulness meditation, choose an environment free of any distractions. You can select a part of your home that is quiet and peaceful. It can be your garage, the place next to the tree house or an empty room. After selecting the place, try to dedicate it to meditation only. Avoid doing other activities there.

Next, soften the ambience to make you feel more relaxed. You can place some flowers or pictures of beautiful places on a table to feel calm when you enter that room. You can even light up some candles (scented, if you prefer), dim the lights, and do whatever relaxes you.

You may find yourself stationary during meditation for several minutes so put on some comfortable clothes so you feel relaxed throughout the practice. Also, check if the room temperature is appropriate and warm/cool enough for you.

Choose a Time to Meditate

Next, decide on a time and duration to meditate. Start slow and then gradually increase the time in chunks. Begin meditating for 5 minutes a day and then gradually add 5-minute sessions every month. Don't burden yourself by setting an hour for meditation on day 1. Also, set a timer to avoid the temptation of checking the time during your meditation.

Sit in a Comfortable Posture

Once you have decided on a place and time to meditate, go to that place at your meditation time, and then sit comfortably. Choose a posture that is the most comfortable for you to sit in. People often associate meditation with sitting cross-legged (lotus position) or sitting in a particular pose. That's not true. There is no right or wrong way to meditate. You can sit on the floor, lie down, or sit in a chair. Try different postures to find out which suits you the most.

Align Your Thoughts with Your Breath

Once you are settled, align your mind with your breath. It takes some time to settle in and let go of your emotions. You may notice that your mind is dancing up and down. You feel emotional as all the unpleasant experience of the past or tensions of the future erupt in your mind. This is normal and everybody who is new to meditation feels the same. Just keep all the thoughts flowing in your head and don't be judgmental about them.

Now start taking deep breaths and feel the air pumping in and out of your lungs. While doing this, you may notice that a negative thought crosses your mind. Stop engaging with it; try to focus on your present. Focus on your breath as you inhale and exhale the air. Focus on your body and your surroundings.

This practice helps you to live in the present and to observe your thoughts from an unbiased and neutral perspective. When you treat your thoughts as the air, which enters and goes out of your lungs without affecting them, you start to live in the present and don't become bothered about your past or future. As a result, you stop being anxious all the time and don't feel stressed at all.

That's one way to train yourself to live in the present. There are other ways to practice mindfulness. In the following chapter, we will look at Body Scan Meditation.

Chapter 12: Body Scan Meditation

Beginner's Body Scan Meditation

This chapter is going to be a bit different, as you can probably tell. While we have discussed the various types of meditation, there has never been a title called 'beginners' anything. That is because while yes, we do have to all learn things for the first time, but the meditations don't really change that much.

The longer your practice the previous meditations, the better you become at it, but the process does not really change that much. The postures stay the same. The process stays the same. You just get more adept and dig deeper into the mind and thoughts. That is why this meditation should start with a beginner's body scan meditation, so here we go.

Try this meditation practice to relax your body from head to toe. Body scanning is also called 'sweeping the body'. It is a fundamental part of any mindfulness meditation, but the purpose is more body-centered than mind and thought centered. You will explore how every part of your body feels, from the top of your head to the tips of your toes. Here's the catch 22. If you notice anything that is uncomfortable, you won't do anything about it. You can scratch and itch. You can't squirm. You can't move a part that has that pins and needles sensation of falling asleep. Your only job is to notice it.

The meditation is usually done by lying down in a comfortable position. Then you mindfully and slowly notice your body as your mind moves from each part of your body. While this can be very relaxing, it also supports making the mind-body awareness that is needed in all the previous types of meditation discussed.

Also, as in the other meditations, you will be practicing the skill known as unattached observation and mental noting. The thoughts that arise should be noted while you continue to breathe and notice any input from your other senses. After acknowledging them, gently guide your awareness to the next body part.

In this body scan technique of meditation, the parts of the body you focus on become the objects of your meditation. Remember the sitting open eyes meditation with the candle? It is the same principle, except your body parts, become what you return your awareness too when your mind wanders.

This meditation is helpful because we sometimes inflict unintentional stress on our bodies through bad posture or other unhealthy habits. Slouching can cause stress on the spine. By the same token, but in the opposite direction, we often overextend the corrective action, and that too can cause discomfort.

Habitual unhealthy eating causes stress on many organs, as does smoking. The practice of body scanning can bring these problems to your attention and you can actually work to change it. For instance, if you do a body scan and notice a tightness in your right shoulder, you first release that tension, by relaxing the muscles and taking deep breaths.

The assessment phase begins when you ask why you have that tension in your shoulder. Your subconscious mind will send thought that will try to help you figure it out. The answers may not come right away, but over time, you will come to understand more of what your thoughts are trying to tell you.

Body Scan Benefits

Body scan meditations is a simple way to practice a technique that has many applications. In yoga, for instance, the human body is mapped in chakras. Chakras are energy centers that are mainly along the spinal column. These points control the flow of energy and certain physical functions, spiritual centers, physical function, and emotional reactions.

In Chakra Balancing meditation, which happens to be one of the most popular of the body scan meditations, one guides one's awareness through the seven main chakras, taking a moment to feel and consider each energy center. The physical health is considered to associate with these chakras and the daily life we experience as well.

Releasing tension that arises while doing this meditation and releasing with breathing techniques and mentally letting go of any stress will unblock the associated chakra.

Deep relaxation and improved sleep: you will practice keeping your mind alert and, at the moment while allowing the body to decompress deeply into an effortless stillness.

Alleviation of insomnia: During this meditation, you will be alert, but your body will be systematically relaxed, part by part, and thus allowing you to fall asleep.

Mind-body connection. Each part of the body will join into the practice as you go. As you highlight each part, your conscious awareness will be directed at a single body part at a time so that you can feel what is going on with it. The goal of meditation is to listen to the signals the body is sending you. To actually witness and acknowledge what it is saying to you.

Self-awareness and self-regulation: you can become more aware of yourself and how you process emotions. If you find you are becoming frustrated, your tone sharper, and the muscles tighten in your neck and shoulders, you have the chance to use your awareness to choose the right words and actions that are in your and everyone else's interest under the circumstance.

Deeper Meditation: The more we focus on the body in this meditation, the less we will have to do so in other types. It's like clearing the body so you will not have to do so during other meditations.

Equipment you will Need:

☐ A comfortable place big enough to lie down. Preferably on your back, using a mat or rug, with a pillow under your head, a pillow under your knees, and a light blanket on top of you. A bed is not recommended unless you are using the meditation to fall asleep.

☐ A quiet space to lie where you won't be easily distracted

☐ A timer. (As usual, if you are using your cell phone, turn off the notifications, and put it on vibrate.)

☐ Your meditation notebook, a pen or pencil

Getting Started

This is simply an introduction to this technique. As with most things, one should start with the basic concepts and once those are learned, proceed to the next level and so on.

☐ Find a place to lie down that is quite

☐ Put one pillow under your head, another under your knees, and cover yourself with a light blanket.

☐ Set your intention: "I am going to commit the next 15 minutes to practice a body scan meditation. I will mindfully guide my awareness throughout my body, release any tension, breathe through any sensations, thoughts or emotions that come up, accept things as they are, and maintain an alert wakeful mind even as my body enters deep relaxation."

☐ Set your time for 15 minutes

☐ Lie down. Get comfortable. Allow your eyes to close,

☐ Concentrate your awareness on your breathing, feeling your lungs expand and contract

☐ Allow your breathing to be the only movement you make.

☐ Notice the different sound and movements all around you.

☐ Bring your awareness to your head, your scalp, your forehead, your cheeks, the musculature of your face and jaw.

☐ With an exhale release any tension or pressure. Take a few deep breaths.

☐ Move your awareness to your neck and shoulders and repeat breathing

☐ Continue down your body in the same way. Your arms, hands, and fingers. Your chest and upper back. Your belly, hips, and lower back, pelvis, and thighs. Keep breathing gently, but deeply in and out through your nose.

☐ Keep moving down through your knees, calves, shins, ankles, and feet, all the way to the very tips of your toes

☐ Rest in stillness. Notice any impulse you feel to wiggle or fidget, but breath through it, letting go of any tension and override the temptation to move around. Accept things as they are.

Finishing Up

When your timer goes off, feel your body's sensations and thoughts that pop up. Take a few deep breaths and slowly begin to move and stretch your body. A lot of time the final pose is called the Shavasana or 'corpse pose'. This is done on your back with your palms facing up. Transitioning means slowly rolling to one side, taking a few breathes, and then lifting yourself up to sitting. It is important to take a moment to gather yourself before getting up and keeping the relaxed state you developed.

Write in your journal when you have the time. Be sure to note things like sensations you felt that you had not expected. What parts of your body stood out the most for you? Did your thought stray to one part of your body more than others?

Digging Dipper

There are seven chakras in the body. Going deeper means concentrating on these chakras in the right order:

Crown Chakra, which is located on the top of the head is associated with the brain stem, the pineal gland and is said to govern the individual's sense of spirituality and connection to a higher power.

Third Eye Chakra, located in the center of the forehead and is the inner eye of wisdom, knowledge, and understanding

Throat Chakra located in the throat is considered to affect the communication and truth

Heart Chakra in the heart center is associated with the connection to others and the world

Solar Plexus Chakra is in the gut and around the severed umbilical cord, where the individual life and free will were first declared from the mother

Sacral Chakra in the sexual organs is associated with creativity in the biological sense and in creative pursuits.

Rook Chakra is located at the base of the spine and is related to home, grounding, stability, and survival

Questions:

Did you notice any difference in the chakras of your body as you performed the scan?

Blocked or partially blocked Chakras can affect your health. When you met resistance in a chakra, did it match with your physical findings?

Often one chakra will come to mind more than others. That usually indicates there is work that needs to be done to change the energy flow. What chakra or body part came to your mind the most while doing this meditation?

Chapter 13: Meditation Principles

The origins of meditation

Meditating does not mean living in a passive state of disconnection from reality; it is an opening to the purity of life, which makes us more lucid, strong, confident and courageous, so that we can stand more firmly in life for what we really want. This "mindfulness" opens our hearts and makes us see reality from the perspective of **SENSE**, that sixth sense that seems to be lacking, disconnected from the modern human. The well-lived spirituality is embodied by a high consideration of our reality, by an ability to say "**NO**" and to assert ourselves.

This pseudo-spirituality that invites us to enter a false security is a trap...It's a decoy intended to mollify all sincere seekers and to divert them from the true path of the Heart, which is in force **ACTION**, determination and inner calm.

Meditation, whatever its form, is one of the pivots of Buddhist practices. It is even one of the key actions.

Meditation through the ages

The history of meditation is lost in the mists of time. What are the commonalities of different meditative traditions, now studied scientifically?

Already, in its etymology, the word **meditate** means one who wants to grasp the meaning. To meditate is to think of something, or to undergo a long and careful consideration. Yet, until the early fifteenth century, meditation meant to reflect on the action of a mysterious religion, a sign that meditative practices were bonded tightly with religion. But the ancient root of the word brings us to the theme of this issue, since the Latin term **Medeor** (found in medicine) means treating. Did the ancient people perceive the subtle existence of a bridge between the meditative practices and their medicinal properties on the body-mind? **Absolutely**.

Why it's important to meditate

Everyone can meditate, whether they are alone in their room, driving their car, in the hospital, with their colleagues at work, in a gym, or cooking and eating. Millions of us now are addicted to this deliberate attention exercise, focusing on what is happening moment by moment, living in the present—without any attention or design

Practicing meditation is a habitual and automatic act, although few people are aware that it is also a unique and personal approach for each volunteer practitioner.

Making the choice of meditating on a certain subject helps to focus attention on positive objects, and on the good thoughts that can influence our minds and even our bodies. This is what we invite with the ancestral and modern spiritual traditions.

Why and how to practice meditation?

The image of meditation may suggest that it is an exotic practice related to Eastern religions; it requires adopting a sitting posture, requiring bending the legs oddly while placing the hands in a strange way. It can also give the impression of a certain "**sacred**" practice. All these ideas are actually false.

Everybody can meditate

In reality, meditation is a choice of focusing the mind on anything in particular. Reading a book, watching a movie, or even focusing on a TV commercial are forms of meditation. Thinking about work or everyday life problems before sleeping every night is actually a form of meditation. Focusing on the fruit that you are purchasing is another form. Therefore, we all practice meditation every day without even noticing we do.

We create our own reality in every moment of life, thinking about and observing our environments. Over time, each person develops thinking habits of their own, and on each particular topic. For example, some prefer watching violent programs on television to meet their anxieties, while others fantasize about their lives through reading novels that talk about a more positive view on life and what it should be, since that is really what people are searching for.

Selecting the object of meditation

Many spiritual traditions use this human tendency to constantly think, absorb information and experiences; to encourage a better life.

And their reasoning is based on:

Since we are always thinking, why not consciously focus the mind on positive and beneficial subjects?

Why not use meditation to learn how to operate our thoughts and emotions and develop positive habits to elevate our mental, physical and spiritual levels?

☐Everyone can develop their potential as human beings, mentally, physically and spiritually.

Practicing meditation to live happier

Practicing meditation is not mystical or inaccessible. It is not just for the elite or for those who are asking to have great knowledge. Meditation is, instead, very down-to-earth and accessible to everyone, without exception. Many meditation forms are inspired by ancient and modern spiritual traditions, which do not impose any faith or belief. Whether or not you follow any spiritual practice, practicing meditation has a single purpose: **to have a happier life.**

How do we meditate?

One must meditate by voluntarily devoting a moment to focus their mind positively. There are many meditation techniques. You can try several methods, then select the one that suits you the best.

These techniques involve four basic technical concepts:

Concentration

Reflection

Visualization

Feeling

To practice meditation during a meeting or when you're busy doing something important, you must apply one or more of these methods during that time. It is important to remember that these techniques are a means to an end; they are not the purpose of meditation, but only tools to use to meditate successfully.

It is not difficult to become a master of mental focus; with experience, one becomes able to sit for hours, entirely focused on their breathing, a sort of spiritual sport. If you do not use your power of concentration to become more positive, kind and compassionate, you miss the essential goal of meditation.

It is therefore important to mobilize your will; before any meditation session, you need to say:

"I would like to meditate today to become happier, kinder, and more generous; to serve others and myself."

When the meditation session ends, you have to say:

"I devote my efforts to the benefit of others and myself."

This end point of meditation has the effect of significantly strengthening the benefits of each session devoted to practicing meditation.

The concentration for meditation

In the first technique, the mind must focus on:

An external object, such as a statute of Buddha, an image of Jesus, or simply a candle or a flower, etc., or an interior object, such as the breath or the heartbeat.

What are the benefits of this technique?

The first benefit of this technique is to soothe the mind and lead to some inner peace. Indeed, the focus on a specific object promotes calm and balance, in addition to stabilizing the mind.

The second benefit comes from the fact that it is difficult to completely stop thinking beyond the meditation of time; our thoughts and emotions produce models that allow us to learn about ourselves.

The third benefit is that this concentration promotes focus on particular topics in everyday life.

The fourth benefit is to prepare the mind for other forms of meditative practices.

The reflection meditation tool

Instead of avoiding thinking to calm and stabilize the mind, you can think of something specific. The selected object can be a problem encountered in life, something that triggers angry feelings, or to develop a virtue such as kindness or compassion.

By voluntarily devoting time to reflect on a particular topic, you will generate a positive change; the mind will be trained to become more assertive. With the gaining of this assurance, the mind can be more assertive not just during meditation, but throughout daily life.

View to meditation

Most meditations demand visualizing something, creating a mental image. Visualization helps to generate reality, to manifest the desires and intentions to change behavior, and expands more to change the bodily processes.

For example, the meditations of **"Tara"** require the visualizing of the feminine aspect of Buddha, who spreads fear and cures diseases. Visualization is indeed extremely powerful tool meditation. With a little practice, expertise improves, and viewing becomes easier and obvious; the benefits of this technique are equally divided between the mind and the body, which will become stronger each day.

Feeling to meditate

Some meditations lead us over a process to collect experienced feelings. For example, when meditating with a partner, you learn to remove the barriers of friendship and intimacy between you. Meditation is scientifically proven to elevate relationships between partners and friends.

Common obstacles to meditation

The most common obstacle that causes us not to meditate is that when we feel good, we feel that we do not need to meditate, because we are too busy feeling good and we have already achieved what meditation is already about. Similarly, when we feel bad, we cannot meditate, because we feel too bad to focus, it takes too much effort, it will be worse if we meditate, etc. There is always a good reason not to meditate. It's similar for practicing sports or eating healthily; we know we should do it, but we hesitate.

The second major obstacle is, of course, time, the precious liquid gold that keeps sliding between our fingers, as it seems. We take a long time to let go of the bad habit of neglecting ourselves without considering the time spent in vein, when in reality, all we really need is to be well centered and reconciled with ourselves.

The only solution to this dilemma is to not ask yourself every day about the time available for meditation, but rather to make it as spontaneous as you possibly can.

Although meditation is a very simple practice, it is not always easy to meditate. Meditation is a life of discipline, an evolutionary path of inner exploration in the heart of the great mystery of self-discovery. All the great spiritual traditions of the world stress the importance and the supreme value of meditation. We cannot escape this truth: if we want to transform ourselves, evolve, and heal, we must first sit down, close our eyes, be calm, and be available and dedicated to meditation.

Chapter 14: Stress And Flow State

We're just midway through the book and already you should have picked up some rather valuable skills. You now understand how to go into a mindful state at any given opportunity to better enjoy your environment or at minimum just to get away from stress for a few moments of reprieve.

But let's rewind and check out that stress in a little more detail. What is it regarding stress that renders it so severe? Why are we attempting to fight stress? And is stress always harmful?

In fact, stress is one thing that is sorely misjudged by plenty of people. Stress is not actually 'one thing'; instead, it is a spectrum of reactions that happen in reaction to harmful situations. Basically, when you spot a threat, your body reacts by discharging hormones and neurotransmitters that set off the 'fight or flight' reaction. This is the reaction that I explained earlier and it is regulated by the following hormones/neurotransmitters (neurotransmitters resemble hormones, but they impact the brain more immediately and don't endure as long):

Dopamine.

Epinephrine.

Norepinephrine.

Serotonin.

Cortisol.

Glutamate.

Testosterone.

Oestrogen.

These then collectively induce a variety of symptoms that you ought to recognize if ever you've gotten involved in an argument, fight or unsafe situation.

These symptoms involve:

Feeling of dread.

Racing considerations.

Trembling.

Muscle contractions.

Vasodilation (expanding of the veins).

Raised heart rate.

Pupil dilation.

Resistance to pain.

Reduction of the immune system and gastrointestinal system so that more blood and materials can be delivered to the brain and muscles.

Raised sensitivity to sounds and illumination.

Shortsightedness.

Fast breathing.

Sweating.

Raised blood thickness to promote the blood to clot just in case of an injury.

Simply put, our body enters into a 'high-performance mode' by redirecting energy and supplies far from upkeep tasks and less immediately critical procedures. Our strength, speed and capability to fight or climb rise and this helps make us more potent and more capable of taking action.

This reaction evolved in the wilderness to serve to help us defend ourselves in the event of danger. If we noticed a predator, or if we found a forest fire, then these adjustments would enable us to escape. Similarly, we would end up being superior fighters when contending with members of our own species for materials.

And in some cases in the contemporary world, this reaction can be precisely what we require. If a thug pulls a knife on you, then this will provide you the ideal opportunity of fleeing to live another day.

Chronic Stress

However, the issue comes when the danger isn't a tangible threat and when it isn't an 'urgent' threat. We just reside in a world that we didn't evolve for and this implies that a lot of our systems are basically outdated.

For instance, if you're giving a speech, at that point, your body will respond in just the exact same way as it would if you discovered a forest fire. And in this instance, none of the modifications would assist at all. You'd be more prone to stuttering, you'd appear sweaty and your voice could even change.

And if you panic (in some cases stress can seem like a heart issue) then this can at some point develop a bad cycle inducing you to get more and more stressed, ultimately hyperventilating and losing consciousness as a result. This is what occurs when it comes to an anxiety attack!

Moreover, this is likewise how we react to owing money, or despising our jobs.

But we can't flee from these issues and we can't combat them. And this then implies that the fight or flight reaction can continue at 'low degree' for a long period of time. This is what we refer to as chronic stress and it's awful for all kinds of reasons.

For starters, chronic stress implies that our immune system and the digestive system are subdued for extended periods of time. This can lead to malabsorption as we become less able to absorb extra nutrients from our food. And it can stop us from resting and make us more prone to the disease.

What's more, is that ultimately, this stress can induce us to 'run out' of the catecholamine neurotransmitters that make it possible for us to concentrate. This is called 'adrenal fatigue,' and it's related to depression and chronic anxiety.

Note at the same time that no neurotransmitter and no hormones operate in a vacuum. If you boost one, you change others. And when you raise cortisol (connected with chronic stress particularly), you also raise ghrelin-- the appetite hormone. This also promotes something referred to as 'lipogenesis' implying that more of the fuel sources in your diet will be kept as fat rather than utilized for energy.

As a matter of fact, cortisol even breaks down muscle by creating something referred to as myostatin which tells the body to break down muscle for energy. So it's vital for your physique at the same time that you find out how not to feel stressed out when it isn't beneficial.

This is why it's so vital that we find out how to react suitably to the scenario at hand and to subdue stress when it isn't suitable, so that we can proceed appreciating life and remaining healthy. Mindfulness is the road to that eventuality.

Positive Stress

But the thing is, there is something such as 'positive stress.' The goal here is not to entirely get rid of stress from your life. Instead, it is simply to manage it.

As we've already observed, stress is a beneficial tool if you're attempting to improve your physical functionality. If you're in a race, or if you're surfing, at that point this reaction is precisely what you require to things done.

But the perfect scenario would be that you get all the perks of the fight or flight reaction, without the downsides. Picture if you could acquire that concentration and that improved muscle mass but in the absence of the sense of dread and fear.

As it occurs, just such a state might exist. This is what psychologists refer to as a 'flow state,' and it has a tendency to be set off during times where we are extremely concentrated on something that we also really enjoy. The example provided frequently is extreme sports, where several athletes illustrate the world appearing to slow down around them whilst they carry out incredible moves and feel more vigorous than they ever have been before.

We also encounter flow when we're entirely concentrated on the work we're performing, or when we're so deep in focus that we neglect the time.

Throughout this state, we create identical neurotransmitters and hormones but with the inclusion of an additional one called 'anandamide'-- the bliss hormone that is also linked to complex and imaginative thinking. It's really the same chemical that offers marijuana its impact but what the majority of people don't know is that it's likewise created organically by the brain.

Keep in mind though that again this isn't truly just 'one state' but instead a spectrum. We could be somewhat stressed and really stressed. We can be somewhat alert or really alert. We could be vigilant and upset, vigilant and joyful or vigilant and scared. It's helpful to think about the brain with regards to 'states' but just understand that there are numerous states in between at the same time and it's more probable that you're someplace here on the spectrum.

Flow states aid us to operate at our best and concentrate more, but they don't induce the same adverse effects as a common fight or flight. The difference?

Satisfaction. So if you are able to attempt and delve into the satisfaction of what you're doing and see it as an enjoyable challenge as opposed to something awful, then you're more probable to enter that flow. Locate the fun in what you're carrying out, find what you're enthusiastic about in it and find out how to really enjoy it. You should do all this utilizing very comparable techniques to the cognitive restructuring we've already noticed.

And also, you also require a low level of 'eustress.' Eustress is the twin of chronic stress but is once again a more desirable type. Eustress is the type of stress that encourages us to do things. For instance, if you have a test turning up and you don't experience any stress whatsoever, then there is a likelihood that you're not going to study for it and therefore, you won't get great marks.

Having just the appropriate amount of low level 'stress' is what you require to ensure you begin studying early and perform the best you can. Eustress doesn't simply have to suggest a negative inspiration. It can also suggest a positive inspiration. It's stress, but it's centered around something favorable.

Delving Into Hidden Powers

Then there's the kind of stress that can uncover additional physical and psychological potential. I'm not stating that anybody is going to manage to practice themselves to the point where they can gain access to this potential; all I'm stating is that it is real which is extremely intriguing and hopefully details the opportunities that are present and the reason why gaining access to more of your brain and your feelings is so extremely powerful.

So keeping that in mind, the first instance is a little something called a 'flashbulb memory.' This shows the potential we have to remember things in vibrant detail if we believe the event is crucial enough. Reflect on where you were at the moment you first became aware of the 9/11 attacks, or maybe where you were the moment you initially found out about Michael Jackson. Additionally, think about a moment that was especially crucial in your own life-- for good or for bad.

The odds are that you are able to recall these events in much more precise detail than you can other aspects of your biographical memory. This is what's referred to as a 'flashbulb memory.' To some extent, this is the result of continued rehearsing: when something significant takes place, we replay it again and again and again in our heads. But it's also the outcome of neurotransmitters being discharged that adjust the way the memory is set and make those links substantially stronger.

And then there's crisis strength. Crisis strength, also referred to as hysterical strength, is the title provided to occurrences where people instantly take advantage of amazing strength. The traditional instance here is the Mom who manages to lift a car off of their stuck child underneath. How is this achievable?

Although there is extremely little in the way of scientific research examining this phenomenon, there is an actual theory regarding how it could work.

Whenever you contract your muscle typically to lift something, your brain transmits signals that journey via your central nervous system and to the 'neuromuscular junction.' Acetylcholine (indeed, the neurotransmitter) is unleashed and this induces muscle fibers to fire. Only we're never very able to recruit 100% of those muscle fibers. Typically, we recruit approximately 30% of them and even a qualified athlete will just manage to get up to approximately 50%.

This is believed to be an evolutionary restriction, the concept being that employing 100% of our muscle would leave us totally drained and prone to attack. Furthermore, it could, in fact, result in injury by putting excessive pressure on our connective tissues and joints.

But to display the type of strength we really have hidden away, just view anybody who receives an electrical shock and gets tossed across the room. This is induced not by the electricity itself but by the person's muscles when they powerfully contract as the reaction to the shock. This induces them to gain access to 100% of their muscle fiber which is sufficient to catapult them all over the room, although they aren't utilizing a jumping technique!

And there's another way we appear to be able to take advantage of increased muscle contraction: by promoting the production of the catecholamine neurotransmitters and fight or flight hormones. It is assumed that under times of extreme stress, we can engage a lot more muscle mass and thus achieve supernatural strength.

And once again this is a range. Really, causing even a small fight or flight reaction is sufficient to somewhat boost your strength in the gym. Studies reveal that if we train with loud noises in the background, or if we train while clamoring (which also promotes the production of comparable hormones) we are really capable of involving additional muscle.

So psyching yourself up prior to a workout just could be among the very best ways to boost your functionality in the gym! Managing, not subduing stress might just be the trick to discovering your full potential.

Chapter 15: Practicing Guided Mindfulness Meditation With Audio Visual Stimulation.

Using audio visual aids enhances mindfulness meditation training and you will find beautiful music videos available created to deepen relaxation states, and you will find that they will lull you into a floating state of consciousness which creates inner peace.

Additionally consider learning and practicing Yoga for more enhanced benefits of mindfulness, meditation and deep transcendental meditation practices.

"The Healing Benefits of These 3 Infinite Practices."

Yoga meditation and mindfulness can be called the 3 infinite practices, or spiritual growth, renewal and harmony of life. Of course they have been around for centuries but dismissed by western culture as religious nonsense.

However more and more people are seeking training in these courses and fortunately with internet technology, they are now readily available online.

You need mindfulness, relaxation and un-jumbling of your life if you are always feeling tired and stressed, suffering a body full of aches and pains when you wake up each morning, having no energy, or having no desire for sex?

The solution to complete body healing is not medicines but using the power of your mind.

People in the western world are now realizing the health benefits of meditation after scientific research with brainwaves and the study of certain groups practicing these techniques have shown incredible all round benefits in their lives.

You can thus rest assured that the psychological benefits of meditation are numerous, the benefits of practicing Yoga beneficial for your body suppleness and fitness, and mindfulness for inner healing as well.

Much research has been done and continues on healing benefits of meditation and even medical doctors are realizing just how powerful the psychological and the physical benefits can be by applying these practices.

As mentioned above regarding training in these practices allows me to point out a wonderful meditation training course that offers complete resources to managing stressful jobs and fast paced lifestyles, time management, family responsibilities, and shows you how to master the healing benefits of meditation is called Dance The Spiral Course meditation.

Scientists and researchers have already proven that brain waves of those that practice meditation are healthier both physically and mentally while also being happier as added benefits.

Practicing the art of meditation can help people feel less anxious and stressed while also allowing them to be more in control of their life, something that is important in today's fast paced lifestyles.

As now mentioned thus far, the healing benefits of meditation are just the tip of the iceberg so if you would like to reach a new level of self awareness, boost your health, and manage your life to live every moment to the fullest practice these techniques and enjoy a life that is fulfilled and happy.

The healing benefits of meditation improve your overall health and well being, and calm your mind and subconscious.

Practicing proper techniques of regular meditation and Yoga, will further help increase blood flow to different parts of the body improving muscle suppleness. The added benefits of this are higher oxygen levels, decreased blood pressure and tension in your muscles and better restful sleep patterns.

The reduction of emotional stress is a further benefit in decreasing those common aches and pains, bad headaches, backaches, and assist with the body to detox ridding itself of the poisons built up from tension and stress.

If you like you can invest in a state of the art 'Dance the Spiral' course which we mentioned above which will show you how to gain maximum healing benefits of meditation and this is all you really need.

There is no fancy equipment needed for practicing meditation but only the proper methodology and a peaceful place where you can completely let yourself go.

To enhance the experience and get full healing benefits of meditation add relaxing music, incense and candles. The practice of simple Mindfulness and Meditation exercises can be done no matter where you are.

What you need to do is teach your mind relaxation techniques, deep breathing exercises and later you can even learn how to do Yoga which is excellent for your body well being.

During mindfulness exercises and meditation calmness will cocoon you and rhythmic breathing with yoga poses sends you into deep meditative states.

Meditation and yoga focus on one part of your body at a time allowing you to release tension and let positive energy flow. During meditation each part of your body is given attention and once you have completed the tour you can focus on your surroundings.

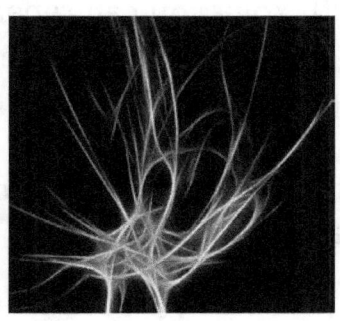

During Yoga and meditation you will feel positive energy flowing from your body and from this you can start focusing on your surroundings.

If you are meditating outdoors you can drink in the beauty of nature by focusing attention on different plants, trees, the sky, clean air or birds and animals.

Change your focus to different objects and hold for a certain period of time and through this you will start a deeper understanding of how you are becoming at harmony with everything.

During the stages of mindfulness and meditation with Yoga you can repeat your focus on any object you choose creating a balance and peacefulness that you never thought was possible. This deeper awareness will open your mind and make mental tasks and decisions clearer.

Mindfulness and meditation is a gentle way to train your mind and with the help of Yoga, soft calming music, or even videos of nature can help you enhance these meditation states.

If you are struggling with stress then your thoughts become jumbled and taking time out for mindfulness and meditation exercise smooth out these wrinkles making everything crystal clear.

Chapter 16: Body And Mind As One

What do you see when you look into the mirror? Where does your attention go to when you come up-close with yourself and come face to face with it? Do you instantly scrutinize that new pimple that popped out yesterday? Or that new found wrinkle that formed overnight from laughing and smiling too much? If you stood there bare naked, would your eyes go straight to that extra belly fat you've been carrying around for a long time or would your attention and the first re-action go to all the parts you love most about yourself? We've all been there and done it and stand guilty as charged. We have trained our eyes and mind to almost automatically set our attention on our "flaws" every single time we look at ourselves.

In theory, our body is made up of flesh, bones, blood and skin that has trillions of cells residing inside with its respective functioning organs working throughout our whole lives for us but in reality, our body is like a sacred temple we were supposed to take good care of religiously. Instrumentally we were "built and designed" to work the same way. To have the 5 important and crucial main gifts that allow us to enjoy life no matter where and when we want to do so.

We just got to tune in and be in harmony with them. We have eyes to see, ears to hear, nose to smell, mouth to taste, and our largest organ---our skin to feel texture and sensations. Yet, we all take these for granted and choose to nit-pick on the most superficial part of us that more often than not, doesn't even serve a functioning purpose, let alone giving us pleasures of any kind. In fact, giving it attention just stirs up, even more, insecurities, doubts, and every possible negative feeling. Some would want a higher nose bridge, smaller nostrils, bigger lips, bigger eyes, and the list goes on.

In order to connect our minds to our body, we got to learn to come to terms with what we've got and embrace its rough edges and the thing about beauty is, it really lies in the eye of the be-holder. If you can't even love yourself just the way you are, how can you expect anyone else to even begin to do so? When you carry negative feelings for yourself and criticize harshly, it will reflect and bounce off right out of your skin quite literally.

In the next chapter, you will learn how you can start to accept, honor and love yourself completely during your meditative sessions making a list of positive aspects of relevant and applicable tasks and experiences that serve you well.

Chapter 17: Benefits Of Mindfulness

Therefore, you may discover negative intuition drops away, bringing about less tension and stress. Wretchedness may lift. Indeed, even torment can cause less enduring when you begin being aware of it instead of battling it or wishing it less.

So that is what really matters to this book, how to manage life's issues and carry on with a fuller, more energetic life by remaining in the present. Basic? Yes. Simple? No.

This book takes you in stages through the act of mindfulness. To start with I talk about a portion of the advantages of mindfulness, for example, enhanced prosperity, a more steady and adjusted personality and a diminishment in stress and nervousness. In part three, Mindfulnesses Practice, you will figure out how to practice mindfulness of the breath, do a body filter and furthermore how to build up your own mindfulness rehearse.

Breath mindfulnesses basically implies sitting serenely and focusing on the breath as well as can be expected for a couple of minutes. This frequently brings about individuals discovering what number of musings they have skipping around in their mind, regularly cliché or self-basic contemplations. Considerations prompt more musings, particularly in the event that you focus on them or trust them. By focusing on some sensation, in the present, unhelpful contemplations are famished of oxygen. Gradually, as the contemplations are not nourished, their impact wagons and regularly the quantity of musings diminish and you feel somewhat more settled and more in charge. Understanding into the brain and its propensities develop. The body examines rehearse, then again, places us in contact with our body, its strains, and stresses. As these are much of the time associated with feelings it gives us the capacity to take in more about our sentiments and specifically to adapt to troublesome feelings better.

Section four talks about why sitting and watching can be so valuable and prompt peace and serenity. It clarifies how unhelpful musings lose their energy and why feeling our emotions works superior to battling or overlooking our sentiments.

While the formal mindfulness practices of breath and body mindfulnesses are exceptionally useful, it is essential to interface them with everyday exercises, and that is the subject of part five. Here, you will figure out how to practice mindfulness in regular circumstances, for example, brushing your teeth or eating a supper. Little mindfulness practices are presented that might be drilled consistently for the duration of the day. This is the more formal piece of the practice, however, it is vital to figure out how to utilize mindfulness in troublesome life circumstances, thus in part six, we take a gander at a couple of these, for example, those promoting melancholy and outrage.

Contemplations, feelings and body sensations are vital parts of the psyche, and section seven shows how these create as a troublesome circumstance advances. Rather than getting overpowered and annoying, this part shows how you can function with every angle to pick up control of your psyche and not enable the circumstance to wind crazy.

Chapter 18: Being Mindful Of Thoughts

We'll often treat our thoughts as if they were actually true. You might have thoughts like 'I'm not good at this, he's a jerk, nobody knows me, or I'm so smart!' But does thinking them actually make them true? When we have a thought repeatedly, it can sometimes turn into a belief. So a belief is just a thought or a number of connected thoughts that we repeatedly have. Beliefs are very often taken as a fact.

For example, some people used to have the belief that the world was flat. Enough people actually thought this or held this assumption that it was assumed to be a fact for many centuries!

When we begin to pay attention to our internal thoughts with curiosity, then we begin to think about what we're thinking about. We can then move away from believing that a thought is a fact.

Then there's this: if the thought does not have evidence to point to it being fact, ask yourself a different question. What does believing this thought do for you? Is it helping or hurting you?

If the answer is that it's hurting you, then move away from the thought. Choose not to get caught up in that thought.

1.Start the activity by being mindful of your breath. Let yourself notice any thoughts that pop into your mind as you're aware of your breaths. Notice and pay attention to and accept these thoughts without judging them. Thoughts are neither positive nor negative, they're just what they are, a thought that you happened to have been having in that moment.

2.You might become aware that you're having trouble thinking about your thoughts, so think about that. You might be thinking that you can't do this well, but that's a thought! Allow yourself to mull over that thought.

3.Some people like the metaphor of allowing their thoughts to float like leaves on a stream or a cloud in the sky. Buddhists like to think of their thoughts as pages written on water.

4.You might notice that at any moment you become aware of a thought, and it passes and is replaced with another. That's what occurs, thoughts come and they go.

5.Now bring yourself back to the awareness of breath and end with that.

Chapter 19: Practicing Your Metacognitive Skills

People who have high levels of mindfulness often have better metacognitive skills. Metacognition is our ability to think about our own thinking processes and our emotions. We use our metacognitive skills to check how our thoughts and feelings relate to our behavior and experiences.

One of the best ways to practice mindfulness and metacognition is by watching a movie. Movies are designed to stir our emotions. Horror movies for instance create the feeling of fear and uneasiness among its viewers. Comedy films on the other hand, create the feeling of excitement.

We often use movies a medium for escapism, making a perfect tool to observe ourselves when we are emotionally engaged in something.

Take these steps to practice your mindful metacognition:

Choose a movie that you have not seen before. Start watching it as you normally would. In the process, you should keep track of your emotions.

When your emotions are at its peak (fear, excitement or sadness), you should pause the movie and examine your feelings. You should identify the scenes in the movie that made you feel that way.

When you have examined your emotions, you should return to watching the movie.

There is also a second variation of this metacognition technique. In this version, you practice your metacognition without stopping your activity. You can follow these steps:

Watch the movie as you normally would. After watching the first half of the movie, you should imagine your soul leaving your body and examining yourself watching the movie.

You should examine your emotions as you observe yourself. You should also identify the scenes in the movie that affected your emotions the most.

These simple exercises will allow you to examine your thought process and your emotions as they are affected by the movie. Most people who use this exercise report becoming more aware of their own emotions. They also report that they are no longer blindsided by their strong emotions.

You can apply the same mindful metacognition technique in any aspect of your life. When you are stressed for instance, you can step back from your busy life and examine how you feel. Using this technique, you can also identify the factors that cause your negative feeling.

When you are angry with someone for example, you can also use this technique to step back from the situation and examine your feelings. You can also identify the factors that are making you angry and deal with them without venting your emotions out towards other people.

Chapter 20: Five Precepts

There are five precepts pertaining to Buddhist teachings that are essentially immoral actions that one should refrain from in their lifetime. Taking part in this five precepts leads to emotional baggage, karma, and an inability to achieve nirvana. In addition to the five precepts that are important for everyone, there are five more that pertain to Buddhist monks. Of course, you do not need to worry about the ones associated with Buddhist monks, but for informative and educational purposes we will discuss those as well.

The Five Precepts

The five precepts are simple to understand and follow and they make complete sense as to why they exist. These precepts are ones that Buddhists believe that all people should refrain from, should they desire to live a life free of emotional baggage. When you partake in these precepts, you expose yourself to the development of excessive emotional baggage that can lead to unhappiness, ill-health, and an otherwise negative or unfulfilling life. The five precepts are:

- Harming living things
- Taking what is not given
- Sexual misconduct
- Lying or gossiping
- Taking intoxicating substances such as alcohol

or drugs

These five precepts are basically the five laws of "what not to do" that Buddhists live by. In doing so, it saves them from an enormous amount of emotional baggage that they may otherwise carry if they were to engage in these activities. When you engage in any of these five precepts, you will end up carrying experiences of misery, guilt, sadness, anger, greed, and ignorance. As you can see, the results of these five precepts contains all of the Three Poisons which Buddhists look to avoid. In mindfulness practice, it makes sense that you too would want to avoid the Three Poisons and therefore activities that would cause them. In addition to the emotional baggage that these experiences bring about, you would also expose yourself to bad karma, potentially even destructive karma that could destroy your good karma and leave you with a lifetime of bad karma.

The Five Additional Precepts for Monks

While you are not expected to become a monk, nor do you need to be in order to have a strong mindfulness practice, it is always interesting to further explore the teachings that you are learning about. In Buddhist traditions, monks have five additional precepts that they must follow, meaning that they have ten in total. Their additional precepts are:

• Eating substantial amounts of food in midday (from noon to dawn)
• Dancing, singing, or listening to music
• Using garlands, perfumes and personal adornments such as jewelry
• Using any sort of luxurious bed or

seating
- Accepting or holding money, silver or gold

The five additional precepts for Buddhist monks seem a bit extreme for those living in modern day society, particularly in the interesting to learn

Western world; however, it is about. When looking at these precepts on a deeper level, they essentially assist the monk in refraining from experiencing greed, anger, or ignorance. They are taught to develop an inner sense of peace, joy, and fulfillment and to maintain it and sustain it in a more powerful way than we may understand. Again, you do not need to partake in any of these five precepts for any reason, nor do you need to become a monk in order to use the powerful teachings within' this book. This added section is merely for your entertainment and understandings! If you are looking to develop a more mindful life, you may wish to consider the reasons why Buddhists monks refrain from these five additional precepts and what these bring about in your life. Are there luxurious things that you enjoy, such as your bed or jewelry, that you may no longer notice anymore due to habitual use?

If You Engage in One of the Five Precepts

The five precepts are essentially a guide in teaching you to live an ethical life. At the very least you should apply these five precepts in order to ensure that you are living life ethically and without the intention of doing harm or ill-will to yourself or anyone else in this lifetime or any other lifetime. If you were to engage in one of the five precepts, you would experience an incredible amount of emotional baggage and karmic build up as a result. Crossing the five precepts would lead you into unethical or immoral territory, which would naturally lead you into immoral karma. You would inevitably experience bad vipaka as a result. In addition to your bad vipaka, you would also experience emotional baggage that would lead you away from nirvana. You would then need to put forth all of the extra mindfulness work to retrace your steps and lead you back into a path of purity and peace to restore all that you lost when you crossed the ethical ways of life.

The five precepts are set up to help you lead an ethical life that will assist you in carrying good karma and a pure mind, heart, body and soul. When you lead a life in alignment with the five precepts, you ensure that you are going to have a positive existence with long term gratification and fulfillment. You eliminate the emotional baggage and bad karma that arises as a result of crossing the five precepts, which is something that is commonly done in western culture. As a result, you increase your mindfulness practice and lead yourself closer to nirvana.

Chapter Summary:

• The five precepts are five ethical rules of life

- The five precepts include: do no harm, do not take what is not given, do not engage in sexual misconduct, do not lie or gossip, and do not take intoxicating substances.
- Buddhist monks have five additional precepts in their way of life
- You do not have to be a Buddhist or a monk to follow these rules and gain value from them
- These five rules have a powerful ability in reducing and eliminating emotional baggage and bad karma

Chapter 21: Reaching Weight Loss Goals

It is periodically necessary to set goals for losing weight, and for some, this is a greater task than for others. Regardless of whether you need to lose a few pounds, or much more, you will need to find a way ensure that those goals are met and kept to. Several techniques can guide you on your journey to weight loss, no matter what your goal or how quickly you want to lose it.

How can mindfulness help in reaching weight loss goals?

Mindfulness reduces the stressors in your life, which directly impact your weight. Stress leads to anxiety and depression, which are known to cause weight gain. Even with anxiety or depression in your life, mindfulness techniques can help center and balance your energy and moods. This enables you to stay focused on losing weight, and prevents you from becoming discouraged.

Can mindfulness help in losing larger amounts weight?

Mindfulness applies to any weight loss goal, but more importantly, it enables you to maintain your goal weight without gaining it all back. Basic mindfulness techniques help with weight management, and also help develop self-control. Mindless eating plagues many people, and paired with stress, is the main contributor to weight gain. Mindfulness does not replace a healthy lifestyle, but by reducing stress and building self-control, it can lead to one. Do not become discouraged if you do not see immediate results, rather, be patient and press on. The weight will come off and stay off with time and dedication.

What mindfulness practices are best in helping weight loss?

Being mindful of your eating habits is one of the best ways to lose weight. Oftentimes, people fail to notice exactly how much and how often they eat. Casual snacking, particularly of potato chips or other unhealthy options, adds up over the course of a day. Suddenly, after putting many unnecessary calories into their bodies, they have gained weight. Being mindful of these and other eating habits will ensure that you are able to control your portions, enjoy foods without over consuming, and stay away from unhealthy options.

Consider mindfulness of your eating habits as the act of eating with all five senses. Begin by choosing small portions of a food, and sit down with it comfortably. Close yourself off to external distractions. If necessary, begin with a short mindfulness of breathing session. Take the food and smell it, making sure to appreciate the scent of the food. Concentrate on physical sensations, the textures and temperature of the food. Use your eyes to become mindful of the food's appetizing qualities. If the food is lightly sizzling, or produces any sound, try to appreciate those qualities as well. Once you have become mindful of what you are about to consume, taste it in small bites.

Always try to bite into foods in little segments, no matter what the original size of the food piece. Savor each bite, and chew as slowly as you can. By eating slowly and contemplatively, you should be more satisfied than you would by mindlessly eating. Concentrate and focus on the lingering aftertaste, then transition back to mindfulness of breathing. Practicing this mindfulness of eating keeps you from the mindless eating that leads to weight gain. In addition, you will enjoy and appreciate every meal far more than you would have ordinarily.

Is mindfulness of eating enough to replace exercise?

Mindfulness of eating can change your mental state towards eating, and get you started on meeting your weight loss goal, but it cannot replace proper diet and exercise. Exercise boosts your metabolism, allowing you effectively burn calories and process food. While mindfulness of eating may influence the calories that come in, it does not mean that you do not need to also shift your dietary preferences. Eating smaller amounts of bad foods does not effectively cut weight the way that eating larger portions of healthy foods does. In short, mindfulness of eating should be paired with a proper diet and exercise, for a full and sustainable reduction in weight.

Are results fast, or does weight loss through mindfulness of eating take a long time?

In all cases, true and sustainable weight loss takes a considerable amount of time. While you may not shed pounds over the course of a few days, you will immediately begin to feel more satisfied and appreciative of the process of eating. This leads to less overall consumption, and will ensure that you feel full and healthy instead of lethargic and empty. Eating slowly also lets you know more accurately exactly how full you are, unlike fast and mindless eating, which does not allow enough time for you to realize that you are full.

It is scientifically proven that people who eat too fast also eat too much. Practicing mindfulness of eating at every meal is not necessary, though some people do choose to do so. Be sure to close yourself off to external distractions, as they can easily take away from the exercise and nullify the effects of mindfulness.

In that sense, it is not usually a good idea to eat in front of a TV or electronic device. It is recommended that people trying to lose weight eat at a table, without any distractions. Many people choose to exercise after practicing mindfulness of eating, in order to appropriately burn off the calories, but it is not a critical choice. More important is the positive, healthy attitude that stems from practicing mindfulness. This will give you the energy that you need to exercise effectively, and will lead to long term, sustainable weight loss.

Chapter 22: How Meditation Can Change Your Life

You may be wondering how meditation can change your life. You have read about all the benefits and all about what you will feel but why will you feel like that and what do you need to do to be aware of the changes. The fact is that you will find life is more peaceful. The major reason for this is that you tend to look at life from a different perspective, by taking judgment out of the picture. You notice more and are more creative and if you want proof of that, you need to look at what goes on inside the brain. As you grow from childhood to adulthood, you have all different concepts thrown at you in all directions. Teachers tell you certain things, your parents tell you different things and then you go out into the workplace and you learn even more. All the time, the brain filters all of the thoughts and perceptions that you have and stores the significant memories in the subconscious mind. But what if there's too much going on in your mind? This overworks the brain and makes it stressed, sending signals out that allow the release of cortisol, as I have already explained. But there's a lot more going on in the brain than that.

The area nearest to the ear is called the temporal lobe. The occipital lobe is the small area at the back of the brain. Then you have the frontal lobe and the upper area, which deals with sensory things and the motor ability of the human body. But of course, it's much more complex than that. Scientists looked into what happens when people meditate using MRI scans and what's interesting is that the frontal lobe is inactive during meditation. In other words, it stops processing information from the world around you and has time to sleep. But the interest doesn't stop there. Of course, this means that your brain is resting its logical processes, but other parts of the brain start to react in different ways. Beta waves are reduced, putting less pressure onto the mind. If you have ever over-thought something and have caused yourself to feel ill because of it, you will understand that this is the frontal lobe trying to juggle too much information. Try to imagine a room full of boxes that are opened and their contents strewed so that you can't get through the room, let alone look for a specific item. That's what the area of the frontal lobe looks like when you overthink things.

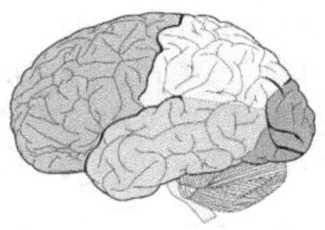

The frontal lobe is that area of the brain that processes information from your life and tries to make decisions based upon the information sent to it. You may have suffered from stress headaches in the past and this is the area most likely to cause it, but meditation effectively switches this area off. Imagine it as a computer that has been unplugged. In the parietal lobe, where you sense things like hot and cold or anything to do with senses, this area also slows down during meditation, so you are unlikely to feel things like discomfort or pain. Thus, you can see that meditation would help someone to reduce their pain and to feel better about life in general. The thalamus in the brain is the area where information is filtered through to the deeper parts of the brain and when you meditate, the flow of information is limited so that instead of having a whole sea of information flowing through your mind, it's reduced to a trickle.

When you meditate on a regular basis, all of the slowing of the information in the brain doesn't just stop while you are meditating. It clears the way for clarity of thought even after you have meditated, if you carry this out on a regular basis. That means pain relief can be lasting. It also means that a feeling of wellbeing and energy can and will follow you through your day. Neuroscientist, Sara Lazar, was in a similar situation to you. She needed to use meditation to help her with her movements since suffering injury and being told that she could not take part in a marathon. She used a class in yoga to help her and was surprised at the changes that she found in the way that she approached life and related to other people. Now, this is a scientist. It's someone who is accustomed to dealing with fact rather than feelings but when she delved deeper into why she was feeling good, she found that meditation helped the neuroplasticity of the brain and that although she had been dubious about her teacher's claim that she would feel better in herself after having practiced meditation, she became optimistic, based upon the way that she began to feel.

It actually surprised her to find that even after a few weeks, the way that she looked at the world changed. She was more compassionate and she spent more time listening to other people's points of view and that judgment had been taken out of her way of life. That surprised her. Being a neuroscientist, she was rather amazed at what breathing in a certain way and meditating was capable of doing and wanted to take her studies further.

There were several studies about how meditation helped to change the way that the brain looked in people who meditated and those who did not. Would there be differences? Remember, this research was done by someone who didn't actually believe that meditation could have a physiological impact on the way that the brain is shaped or performs.

When she took her studies further, and took MRI scans of people who meditated regularly and those who did not, what she found was that the neuroplasticity of the brain remained young in even those of more than 50 years, through the process of meditation. In fact, meditation was acting as exercise for the brain, keeping the subjects' brains young, rather than going through the normal shrinking process associated with old age. Not convinced that the first set of scans had distinguished anything other than differences between certain people, they tried the experiment again, this time carefully selecting people with no previous experience of meditation, who were picked specifically and who went through training in mindfulness meditation for the first time, over a period of eight weeks. The scientists were amazed at the results because the activity in the hippocampus area of the brain was increased. This area is used for regulation of emotions as well as for learning and retention and the scales were loaded on the side of those who meditated as opposed to those who did not. This meant that they were less likely to suffer from the effects of depression and mood swings and had better control over their emotions.

There is another area just above your ear called the Temporo Parietal junction, which showed activity, and it is this area of the brain that deals with compassion. The amygdala area of the brain, by contrast, which is the area that deals with your responses to emergencies and that triggers the fight or flight reaction humans use to protect themselves actually slowed down in activity and shrunk. This was due to the meditation but what's interesting to note is that this wasn't caused by internal stresses. This was caused by external factors. Thus, those who meditate are better able to cope with external stresses and are less prone to anxiety and depression. You can see the full video here.

The way in which meditation changes your life is astounding. It makes you less stressed and therefore able to enjoy life more. It makes you more aware of the world around you and less likely to be stressed by events within your life that are usually seen as stressful. In fact, your responses will be better because you are not adversely affected by things that would normally upset the balance of your life, in that the brain is better able to deal with them, instead of invoking the fight or flight response. You tend to look for solutions to problems, rather than problems arising from problems, and that makes a huge amount of difference to your demeanor.

We already know that there are health benefits to meditation, since we have a chapter devoted to this, but what if I told you that meditation can keep you feeling younger? Well, the above video may just convince you that it can. Meditation changes several things about your approach to life and mindfulness backs up those changes, so that you live in a different way embracing compassion, forgiveness, the ability to think independently of emotions and become more flexible in your approach to life.

Throughout this book, we have praised meditation and mindfulness for good reason and have backed it up with references so that you can see that none of this is just talking about maybes or hypothetical improvements. Even people who meditate for as short a time as 30 minutes a day feel the improvement in their lives. It's important to note that even if you miss a day of meditation, as long as you go back to it and stick to it, you may actually be improving your longevity!

The things that you will notice within the first month or so are mind altering. You will have no doubt that meditation is helping you because you will feel less stressed, more organized and happier within yourself. However, as emphasized all the way through this book, judgement is something you need to remove from your life. It's easy to look at a beggar and think that he is there because he deserves to be, but you do not know his story. Compassion plays a wonderful part in dropping judgement and so does empathy. Each time that you find yourself in a situation where you would normally make a judgement, ask yourself why you think that you have the right to make a judgement, because this is the part of your behavior that is making you unhappy, rather than the thing being criticized. When you learn empathy and can place yourself in the shoes of another person, it opens up a whole world of understanding that is not possible when you close yourself off and judge people.

You will also find that your life runs in a smoother way. It may make very little sense, but instead of being your normal self, you become a better self. You find that you are happier, feel that you have purpose in life and open yourself up to creative solutions to life's problems, so that nothing becomes too much for you. It's a good idea to cut down the amount of influence you have from social media and television and use this time for quiet reflection, or perhaps reading. Some reading material that I can recommend would be "The Prophet" by the Lebanese Philosopher, Khalil Gibran and also works by Rumi. These are inspirational and will enthuse you about life in general. When people become spiritually aware, they also feel much more at peace with life in general. It's hard to feel that peace when you fill your life to brimming with stuff or with activities, but when you meditate, you find that you have a sense of purpose and do not need all of the trappings of the 21st century. You are kinder toward people and feel more satisfied with your life.

This chapter is all about how Mindful meditation makes you feel. In truth your approach to mindfulness meditation counts for a lot. You need to make up your mind that this is what you want for your future. All I can do is tell you the benefits, but I cannot be there to guide you when you go through doubts. However, I can tell you that life will change considerably and that you will care more about your life, and are thus more likely to keep to the routine of meditation and use mindfulness to keep your intuition honed and your senses alive to all the changes that are happening around you all of the time. You will feel yourself grow in stature but what does that mean? It doesn't mean you will earn more or anything of that nature. It just means that you will accept who you are without question and enjoy being a part of your life, instead of being absent from it and then living with the regrets that this absence brings with it.

Conclusion

Mindfulness practices are a great way to relieve you from the burden of stress and worry that currently plague you. While your beliefs and mental traps trigger stress within you, as you progress forward with your practice, you'll find that the real enemy lies deep within your mind and this is your ego.

What is your ego and why does it cause suffering? Well, the ego can be thought of as a perverse self-image. It isn't the same self-image that sits in your unconscious mind. The ego is instead an amalgam of various "shoulds" and beliefs that you have and morphs into something that has a desperate need for an identity.

Understand that the ego doesn't have a need for a specific identity, it just needs something. Its aim is to create a contrast between itself and the surroundings it's in. So, if you've suffered an insult, it seeks to right this wrong by placing you (itself) above the entity that directed the insult at you.

The contrast that is created between itself and the environment need not be a positive one. In other words, it doesn't seek to place itself above the aggressor or trigger of the insult. Even a negative position with regards to your ego will do. This contrast creates an identity of either being better than something or of being a victim.

This is why feeling sorry for yourself never works and is a terrible coping strategy. It is simply your ego fueling itself, and at the end of the day, the ego isn't concerned one bit with where you end up. It needs emotional drama to sustain itself and things like contrast and time provide it with ample fuel.

Mindfulness insists that time is just the present moment but to the ego this is heresy. After all, the current moment is not fixed. It is fluid and therefore impossible to mold and carve an identity out of. It is much better to create the past and the future. These moments are fixed because they have already occurred or because they are projections of a definite goal.

Hence, the ego can draw identities from it. Things like regret and depression originate from the ego ruminating over the past and elation and unbounded thrill arise from contemplating the future. Mind you, it can work the other way around as well. This sort of time travelling is common with the ego and it is all in pursuit of an identity.

This is the "I" that I referred to previously. Mindfulness helps you let go of your need for this "I" and you stop connecting things to yourself and emotionally reacting to events and triggers. Once the "I" is deactivated, everything just becomes an event. That's it.

There's no greater meaning to be sought and the present becomes the only place in time which makes sense. All of the practices outlined in this book aim to help you release this "I" and become one with yourself. New age spirituality focuses on the ego quite a lot and tries to dissect it with the aim of understanding it.

Ancient Buddhism simply chalks it up as existing and then moves onto the solution. It is true that Buddhist texts spend an inordinate amount of time talking about suffering and desire and so on, but the majority of the philosophy is related to practice and discovering truth.

Your formal practices are all a reflection of these ancient Buddhist techniques and your informal techniques are simply a reflection of how life ought to be lived. Remember that all of your mental ticks and pain points are reflected in your body. So, connecting with your body via observing your sensations is of paramount importance.

Initially, it will be tough to put this into practice but after a few weeks, you will notice the improvement in your quality of life. It is at this point that a curious thing happens. A lot of people begin clinging onto this additional feeling of happiness, so to speak, and as it disappears, begin to crave it. This is simply falling prey to the ego, so you should be aware of and avoid this.

Be happy that you're making progress, but remember progress isn't the point of mindfulness. It is the path that is important. This is where wisdom lies, not at your destination. I highly recommend attending a meditation retreat at some point to receive further instruction in how you can deepen your practice. It will be tough, but there are few more rewarding experiences you can undertake.

Stress is not something you deserve to carry in your life, and you should seek to get rid of it when the opportunity presents itself. Let mindfulness show you the way to peace and happiness.

I wish you all the love and peace in the world and wish you the best of luck for your journey!

www.ingramcontent.com/pod-product-compliance
Lightning Source LLC
Chambersburg PA
CBHW072002070526
44583CB00015B/1299